4-12

**DUE**

MAY 1 1 2012

6-15-12

# EVERY DAY
# A FRIDAY
*Journal*

# EVERY DAY A
# FRIDAY

*Journal*

## HOW TO BE HAPPIER 7 DAYS A WEEK

# JOEL OSTEEN

New York  Boston  Nashville

Scripture quotations noted AMP are from The Amplified Bible. Copyright © 1954, 1958, 1962, 1964, 1965, 1987 by The Lockman Foundation. All rights reserved. Used by permission. (www.Lockman.org). Scripture quotations noted KJV are from the King James Version of the Holy Bible. Scripture quotations noted NASB are from the New American Standard Bible®. Copyright © 1960, 1962, 1963, 1968, 1971, 1972, 1973, 1975, 1977, 1995 by The Lockman Foundation. Used by permission. Scripture quotations noted NIV are from The Holy Bible, New International Version® NIV®. Copyright © 1973, 1978, 1984, 2011 by Biblica, Inc.™ Used by permission. All rights reserved worldwide. Scripture quotations noted NKJV are from the New King James Version. Copyright © 1979, 1980, 1982, Thomas Nelson, Inc., Publishers. Scripture quotations noted NLT are from the Holy Bible, New Living Translation, copyright © 1996, 2004. Used by permission of Tyndale House Publishers, Inc., Wheaton, Illinois 60189. All rights reserved. Scripture quotations noted The Message are taken from The Message. Copyright © 1993, 1994, 1995, 1996, 2000, 2001, 2002. Used by permission of NavPress Publishing Group.

FaithWords
Hachette Book Group
237 Park Avenue
New York, NY 10017

www.faithwords.com

Printed in the United States of America

RRD-C

First Edition: March 2012

10  9  8  7  6  5  4  3  2

FaithWords is a division of Hachette Book Group, Inc.
The FaithWords name and logo are trademarks of Hachette Book Group, Inc.

The Hachette Speakers Bureau provides a wide range of authors for speaking events. To find out more, go to www.hachettespeakersbureau.com or call (866) 376-6591.

The publisher is not responsible for websites (or their content) that are not owned by the publisher.

Library of Congress Cataloging-in-Publication Data
Osteen, Joel.
  Every day a Friday journal : how to be happier 7 days a week / Joel Osteen. — 1st ed.
    p.cm.
  Summary: "The ultimate companion tool to help readers of Every Day a Friday experience a happy and meaningful life every day of the week"—Provided by publisher.
  ISBN 978-0-89296-981-4
  1. Happiness—Religious aspects—Christianity.   2. Spiritual journals—Authorship.   3. Diaries—Authorship—Religious aspects—Christianity.
I. Osteen, Joel. Every day a Friday.   II. Title.
  BV4647.J68O882 2012
  241'.4—dc23
                                                                2011042441

# CONTENTS

# INTRODUCTION

My book *Every Day a Friday* encourages readers to choose joy and happiness in each and every day, even those days marked by life's inevitable challenges. This journal companion for the book offers that same encouragement in daily doses supplemented by inspirational and thought-provoking material. You will find Scriptures, inspirational quotations, selected stories, prayers, and points for contemplation. All are provided to engage you in a process of reflection that will enhance your faith and lead you to positive actions.

My prayer is that you will take a few minutes each day to read the daily entries and to add your own thoughts. If you are facing challenges or difficult circumstances, there are prayers and inspirational quotes to help remind you that God is with you each and every moment.

Journaling has been shown to improve problem-solving abilities. Many people find that using a journal helps them to better assess their thoughts and feelings and to find clarity. The process of putting pen to paper and then seeing your words on the page can help you solve problems while keeping matters in perspective and priorities straight. You may release pent-up emotions in the process, and that is a good thing, too.

Like laughter, journaling also has been proven to relieve stress and to boost the immune system in some people. To gain the full benefits, don't worry about punctuation, spelling, or grammar when making your own entries. Simply let your thoughts and feelings flow.

I pray that you will find the *Every Day a Friday Journal* to be a source of inspiration and encouragement step-by-step in your walk of faith. Happiness comes in many forms, whether it's the satisfaction of a job well done, the warmth of a friend's smile, the sound of a child's laughter, or the serenity that comes in knowing God is present in your life. You have the power to choose joy whether through gratitude, with forgiveness, by serving others, or by doing your best to reflect God's best.

This journal is designed to provide seven weeks of daily inspiration and encouragement. It is best read day to day in a quiet place where you can meditate and contemplate for brief periods, away from the usual distractions. Take your time and enter your own thoughts and encouragements. Once you've gone through it, feel free to begin again. Replenish your spirit and listen for the still, small voice of God's grace and direction.

Your entries can serve as a record of your daily progress. Enjoy the process. Do your best, and God will do the rest. Remember always that happiness is yours to choose each and every day.

# Don't Give Away Your Power

# DAY 1

## Choose Happiness Every Day

*Key Truth*
The quality of your choices determines
the quality of your life.

Whatever challenges you may face, whatever circumstances are weighing you down; you can choose your response. How you live your life is totally up to you. It's not dependent on your circumstances. It's dependent on your choices. Abraham Lincoln said, "Most people are as happy as they've decided to be."

Honest Abe would have enjoyed a recent study that found happiness increases 10 percent on Fridays. Why is that? People are excited about the coming weekend so they decide to be happier. They make up their minds on Fridays to enjoy their lives more.

I challenge you to let every day be a Friday. Give yourself permission to be happy every day. Not just on the weekends. Not just when you have a special event. Not just when you're on vacation.

If you have the right mind-set, you can be just as happy on Monday as you are on Friday. The Scripture doesn't say, "Friday is the day the Lord has made." It says, "*This* is the day the Lord has made" (Psalm 118:24 NKJV; emphasis added).

*This* means Monday, Tuesday, Wednesday, and every other day of the week. You can be happy even when it's raining, when you have to work late, or when you have to do the dishes.

Why don't you make up your mind to be happy every day? You've heard the saying "TGIF. Thank God it's Friday." For you and me it also should be, "TGIM. Thank God it's Monday."

"TGIW. Thank God it's Wednesday."

"TGIS. Thank God it's Sunday."

Another study said there are more heart attacks on Monday than on any other day. So many people just decide that Monday is a stressed-out day. They suffer the Monday morning blues.

When you wake up on Monday morning, don't accept those negative thoughts that come knocking on your door, saying, *It's going to be a hard day and a long week. Traffic will be bad. I've got so much work to do. I just need to make it through the Monday morning blues.* Don't buy into those thoughts.

Instead, say, "Thanks, but no thanks. I've already answered the door and almighty God, the Creator of the universe, has sent me a hand delivery of joy. I know this is going to be a great day!"

Decide that for you, there are no Monday morning blues. Instead, choose the Monday morning *dos* by saying, "I do have a smile. I do have joy. I do have God's favor. I do have victory."

## Consider This

Some days are more difficult than others. But if you program your mind in a positive way, you won't have to drag through certain days just hoping to get to Friday so you can finally enjoy life.

---
---
---
---
---
---
---

In the end, it's not the years in your life that count. It's the life in your years.

—Abraham Lincoln

_____

_____

_____

_____

_____

_____

_____

## What the Scriptures Say

This is the day the LORD has made. We will rejoice and be glad in it.

—Psalm 118:24 (NLT)

It seemed like a dream, too good to be true, when GOD [gave us the victory]...Now, GOD, do it again...so those who went off with heavy hearts will come home laughing, with armloads of blessing.

—Psalm 126 (The Message)

## A Prayer for Today

Father, I say "Thanks but no thanks" to negative thoughts, and instead I say "Thank You for sending me a hand delivery of joy." I know this is going to be a great day!

_____

_____

_____

_____

_____

_____

_____

_____

_____

Each morning when I open my eyes I say to myself: I—not
events—have the power to make me happy or unhappy today.
I can choose which it shall be. Yesterday is dead, tomorrow
hasn't arrived yet. I have just one day, today, and I'm going to
be happy in it.

—Groucho Marx

_____

_____

_____

_____

_____

_____

_____

### Takeaway Truth

I can choose happiness every day, so my attitude
should be: *I'm excited to be alive at this moment.*
*I'm excited to be breathing today. I'm excited about my*
*family, my health, and my opportunities. I have plenty*
*of reasons to be happy right now.*

# DAY 2

## *Treat Every Day as a Gift*

*Key Truth*
You can manufacture your
own happiness.

Years ago, a man traveling by train met a well-to-do couple. The lady was wearing expensive clothing and jewelry. They shared their first-class cabin with the fellow traveler, and it was very comfortable. But from the start the lady did nothing but complain. She complained that the temperature wasn't right, complained that there wasn't enough light, complained that the food wasn't good, and complained that her seat was dirty. She made everyone miserable.

During the journey, the traveler struck up a conversation with her husband. He asked what kind of business he was in. He said he had been in the car industry and God had blessed him in a great way. But he added; "Now my wife, she's in the manufacturing business."

The traveler thought: *That's kind of odd. I mean, she's so dignified and dressed so properly. That just doesn't seem like it fits.*

He asked very curiously, "What does she manufacture?"

"She manufactures unhappiness," the husband said. "She's unhappy everywhere she goes."

You may need to change businesses, not physically but mentally. Get out of the business of manufacturing unhappiness. Quit dwelling on what's wrong. Quit seeing the faults and start seeing the good. Start being grateful for what you have.

As I walked out of the house early one recent morning, I heard all these birds singing and singing so loud and so cheerful. Little birds were chirping and chirping. Big birds were making a melody. It was like they were having a big party. I wanted to say to them, "Hey, birds. Have you read the newspapers lately? Did you see the stock market last year? You're not supposed to be singing, enjoying life. What's wrong with you? You're acting like everything is going to be all right."

What was it with those birds? They know a secret. They know their heavenly Father is in control. They know God has promised to take care of them, so they go through the day singing and enjoying life, regardless of the circumstances.

## Consider This

You attract what you put out. If you complain all the time, you will only attract other complainers and their unhappiness, but if you get up each morning with a song of praise in your heart and sing it all day, you will attract praise, happiness, and joy. So put a smile on your face. Go out determined to enjoy each day.

_____

_____

_____

_____

_____

_____

_____

_____

_____

_____

Happiness calls out responsive gladness in others. There is enough sadness in the world without yours.... Never doubt the excellence and permanence of what is yet to be. Join the great company of those who make the barren places of life fruitful with kindness.

—Helen Keller

_____

_____

_____

_____

_____

_____

_____

_____

_____

## What the Scriptures Say

Be happy [in your faith] and rejoice and be glad-hearted continually (always).

—1 Thessalonians 5:16 (AMP)

We know that God causes everything to work together for the good of those who love God and are called according to his purpose for them.

—Romans 8:28 (NLT)

## A Prayer for Today

Father, I know You are in control and that You will take care of me always, so I will spend my days singing to glorify You, enjoying each moment given me, and not worrying about what I cannot control.

_____

_____

_____

_____

_____

_____

_____

Success is not the key to happiness. Happiness is the key to success. If you love what you are doing, you will be successful.

—Albert Schweitzer

_____

_____

_____

_____

_____

_____

_____

_____

_____

### Takeaway Truth

Blaming your circumstances will not relieve
your unhappiness, but changing them will.
Taking responsibility for your happiness is
the first step to finding joy in each day.

# DAY 3

## *Don't Let Anyone Steal Your Joy*

*Key Truth*

Life is 10 percent what happens to you and
90 percent how you respond.

I had a real nice sports car when I first dated my wife, Victoria. I was in my early twenties and wanted to impress her, so I kept that car spotless. There wasn't a scratch on it. Then I was driving home from Victoria's house late one night and I had an accident. I was proceeding through an intersection. The light was green. Another car going the same direction turned right from the wrong lane and hit the back of my sports car, spinning it around.

After taking a few moments to calm down, I stepped out of my car. I knew the accident wasn't my fault, and I'm naturally easygoing. There is not much that upsets me. I checked my spotless car. The back end was totally destroyed.

About that time the other driver climbed out of his car. It was very dark, but I could see he was probably in his fifties. He started ranting, raving, and cursing, and then he said, "Kid, learn how to drive. I am so mad at you."

I thought to myself, *I'm the one who should be upset. He just turned from the wrong lane.* He was about thirty yards away. I could see he was working up his anger. Then he started running toward me like he wanted to fight.

My first thought was, *Do you want some of this?*

You know that's not true. My real first thought was, *How big is he?*

When he came within fifteen yards, I saw he was twice my size. Right then and there I had a revelation: This was not a battle worth fighting.

I went around to the other side of my car.

You say, "Joel, you mean you were a chicken?"

No, I just wanted to live!

He fit into that category of people who will never be at peace with me. We all need to accept that some just will feel that way about us. They will never see our point of view. We might as well let them go and move on. And even if we could win them over, we'd have to wonder if it would be worth it. *What is this going to accomplish?*

What if I had stood up to the guy whose car hit mine and showed him what I'm made of? Big deal. I didn't even know the man. He'd been in my life for less than ten minutes. Trying to make peace with him was not worth the effort. I made a decision that I was not going to give him my power, my joy, or my peace. I stayed away from him and let him cool off. Then we exchanged information and we let the insurance companies handle it from there.

Go into each day positive, hopeful, and expecting God's favor. But at the same time be realistic, knowing that most days will not go exactly as you planned. If you become stressed because you are off schedule, frustrated because someone offended you, or upset because your child wouldn't eat breakfast, you are giving away your power.

It's good to have plans, but at the first part of every day, submit those plans to God and just say, "God, this is what I would like to accomplish today. But I know You're in control, so I submit my plans to You. And I've decided in advance that no matter what comes my way, I will stay in peace, knowing You are directing my steps and that all things will work together for my good."

But too many people these days have the wrong approach to life. They think they can't be happy unless they control all their circumstances and everything goes their way. But that's not realistic. You have to come to the place where you can say, "I don't have to have my way to have a good day. My plans don't have to work out for me to be happy. Everybody doesn't have to treat me right for life to be enjoyable. I have already made up my mind: No matter what does or doesn't happen, I will stay in peace and enjoy this day."

No circumstance can take your peace. No interruption can take your enthusiasm. You have to give it away. The next time you're tempted to be upset and frustrated, ask yourself, *Is this worth giving my power away?*

Jesus said: "Do not let your hearts be troubled and do not be afraid" (John 14:27 NIV). Notice that it's a choice we have to make. Jesus didn't say, "I will make sure your circumstances are perfect. That way you can be happy."

He said, in effect, "The things upsetting you right now don't have to upset you. The people aggravating you, even if they don't change, they don't have to aggravate you." If you'll make adjustments and change your approach to life, you can be happy in spite of those circumstances.

## Consider This

Stop allowing negative people and disappointments and inconveniences to steal your joy. You have to put your foot down and say, "This child gets on my nerves—I love him—but I'm going to rise above it. I won't let this control me." Or, "This grumpy boss jumps down my throat for no reason, but I'm not going to let him ruin any more of my days." That's what it means to not give away your power.

_____

_____

_____

_____

_____

_____

_____

_____

The happiness of a man in this life does not consist in the absence but in the mastery of his passions.

—Alfred, Lord Tennyson

_____

_____

_____

_____

_____

_____

_____

## What the Scriptures Say

May we shout for joy over your victory and lift up our banners in the name of our God. May the LORD grant all your requests.

—Psalm 20:5 (NIV)

The LORD is my strength and my shield. I trust him with all my heart. He helps me, and my heart is filled with joy. I burst out in songs of thanksgiving.

—Psalm 28:7 (NLT)

## A Prayer for Today

Father, I put my trust in You, and with Your help I will not allow anyone to take away my joy. Instead, I will go out each day and expect Your favor.

_____

_____

_____

_____

_____

_____

_____

_____

No cloud can overshadow a true Christian but his faith will discern a rainbow in it.

—Bishop Horne

_____

_____

_____

_____

_____

_____

_____

_____

### Takeaway Truth

Every day we have plenty of opportunities to be upset, to be frustrated, and to be offended. Life is full of inconveniences. There will always be interruptions and difficult people. You can't control all of your circumstances, but you can control your reactions.

# DAY 4

## Express Your Joy

*Key Truth*

Handling difficult people with grace and good
humor disarms them and builds your character.

I went for barbecue one day and the drive-thru lady was very grumpy.
She jumped down my throat before the first part of my order was out
of my mouth.

"Hold on! I'm not ready," she barked.

Then I made the mistake of asking her what the side dishes were.
You might have thought I'd asked for her favorite child.

She screamed the complete list of sides at me, and I'm telling you,
"baked beans" never sounded so scary.

I had to keep reminding myself to stay calm: *You're the pastor of
a church. Keep your joy. Don't let her affect you. Infect her instead.*

You have to talk yourself down in the heat of battle. Giving her a
piece of my mind would have been easy. I'd just repent later. Instead,
I remembered that dealing with challenging people helps build
character.

I placed my order as nicely as could be at the drive-thru speaker. I
said "Please" and "Thank you" and tossed in a "Have a good day!" at
no extra charge.

Then when I drove up to her window, I put on the most fake smile
you've ever seen.

"Good to see you," I said, as chipper as I could muster.

I was really thinking, *You need counseling!*

Grumpy turned from the register, looked at me, and did a double take.

"Pastor Joel, I watch you all the time!"

I wanted to say, "Do you ever listen?"

Then, instead of my barbecue, she handed me one of my books. (I'm positive she hadn't read it yet!)

"Would you sign this for me?" she asked, a little nicer but not much.

I opened it and thought about underlining all the lessons on joy.

Instead, I signed it, "Keep smiling that beautiful smile, Joel Osteen."

And then I drove out of there as fast as I could before her grumpiness spoiled my brisket.

You and I are supposed to be happier than the average person. God has anointed us with the oil of joy. You can't let anyone's bad attitude ruin your good one. Instead, infect them with a smile and a kind word. God knew you would have to deal with negative people. That's why He said "I've given you an advantage; I've anointed you with the oil of joy so you can be happier than those around you."

Tap into that joy and don't hide it. It should be seen.

Studies have proven that a smile on your face is good for you and everyone around you. In one test people were asked to show facial expressions for fear and anger. Their bodies responded just as if they were really feeling those emotions, triggering increased heart rate, raising their skin temperature, and making them sweat. Those same people were then asked to smile, and their heart rates settled down, their temperatures dropped, and they didn't sweat so much. They said they felt happy.

Our Creator knows all this, of course. God talks about our countenances more than fifty times in the Scripture. You see the word *rejoice* again and again. To rejoice doesn't just mean to sing. It also means to brighten up, to put a smile on your face, to be cheerful. When you go through the day with a smile, you are rejoicing. By having a cheerful countenance, being friendly and fun to be around, you are giving praise to God.

Too many people drag through the day with long faces. Some don't smile for months. Then they'll come up with those same sour faces after a service and say to me, "I've got the joy of the Lord."

I'll think: *You should notify your face!*

The Bible says to be sober-minded, not sober-faced. You receive back what you project. If you're sour, grumpy, and unfriendly, then others will be sour, grumpy, and unfriendly back to you. Misery loves company. If you look miserable, you will attract defeat, negativity, gloom, doom, and discouragement.

But when you smile and project an aura of warmth, kindness, and friendliness, you will attract warmth, kindness, and friendliness. Happy people will be drawn to you.

You may have many challenges. I'm not making light of your circumstances but Jesus said, "In the world you have tribulation and trials and distress and frustration; but be of good cheer" (John 16:33 AMP). I've found that sometimes you have to smile by faith. Instead of being depressed, discouraged, or worried, say, "I'm not moved by what I see; I'm moved by what I know, and I know this is the day the Lord has made. I'm going to choose to be happy."

Smiling improves your attitude. You see life in a different light. It's difficult to smile and be negative. It's hard to stay in a bad mood if you act cheerful and friendly. One expert says smiling tricks the body into feeling good. That's the way God created us. Smiling resets your mood.

## Consider This

If you're not receiving what you like, check what you're sending out. No happy person wants to be around an old stick-in-the-mud. Anyone who is going places will avoid the company of people wallowing in the pits. Your happier friends might pull you out of the pit a few times, but eventually they will find more upbeat people with whom to share their lives.

_____

_____

_____

_____

_____

_____

_____

_____

Laughter is the closest distance between two people.

—Victor Borge

_____

_____

_____

_____

_____

_____

_____

_____

## What the Scriptures Say

You love justice and hate evil. Therefore, O God, your God has anointed you, pouring out the oil of joy on you more than on anyone else.

—Hebrews 1:9 (NLT)

Let all who take refuge in you be glad; let them ever sing for joy. Spread your protection over them, that those who love your name may rejoice in you.

—Psalm 5:11 (NIV)

## A Prayer for Today

Father, I know this is the day You made, so I choose to be happy.

_____

_____

_____

_____

_____

_____

_____

_____

_____

Where others see but the dawn coming over the hill, I see the soul of God shouting for joy.

—William Blake

_____

_____

_____

_____

_____

_____

_____

_____

_____

*Takeaway Truth*

When you smile, you send a message to your
whole body that says, "God's in control,
everything is all right. This will be a good
day." Don't wait to see how you feel before
you express your joy. Put a smile on your
face first. Then the joy will come.

## DAY 5

# Bloom Where You Are Planted

................................................

*Key Truth*
No matter your circumstances,
you can rise above them.

................................................

**M**any unfair things happened to Joyce when she was growing up. Her first marriage to an abusive, unfaithful man didn't last. She married a second time and made her husband miserable. She wasn't trying to be a bad wife, but she had just been through so much pain. She was hurt and messed up.

She couldn't trust anybody. She was very negative, critical, and hard to get along with. Her second husband, Dave, wanted to leave her a thousand times. He had every right to walk away. Nobody would have blamed him. But deep down he knew he was supposed to stay. It was the most difficult thing he had ever done. Month after month, even year after year, he was uncomfortable.

His situation was unfair and difficult, but Dave kept blooming where he was planted. He just kept being his best: kind, forgiving, patient, overlooking things. He felt like he gave and gave and never received; all sowing and no reaping.

I'm happy to tell you that today it's a different story for this couple. Dave paid the price. He stuck with her. And now, thirty-five years later, he's reaping great rewards. That lady, his wife, is Joyce Meyer.

She's not only healthy and whole, but they have a ministry touching people around the world.

Joyce and Dave are incredible people. Good friends whom I love and respect. Joyce once asked, "What if Dave would have been like my first husband and taken the easy way out? What if he had not stuck with me and paid the price?"

Sometimes God will ask us to put up with things to help another person. Where are the people unselfish enough to say, "God, I trust You. It's uncomfortable. It's not fair. I'm not doing it because I want to. I'm not doing it because I feel like it. But God, I'm doing it unto You"?

God rewards people like that!

The apostle Paul put it this way, "I have learned to be content whatever the circumstances. I know what it is to be in need, and I know what it is to have plenty. I have learned the secret of being content in any and every situation, whether well fed or hungry, whether living in plenty or in want" (Philippians 4:11–12 NIV).

He was basically saying, "I just bloom wherever I'm planted. I'll be happy and have a good attitude knowing that God is directing my steps. He's in complete control. And it's all a part of His divine plan for my life."

Like Dave, you don't have to allow a bad environment to affect your happiness. Don't focus on the weeds. You may be spending all your time, so to speak, trying to pull up the weeds. In other words, trying to fix everything in your life, trying to make people do what's right, trying to straighten out all your co-workers.

You can't change people. Only God can. If somebody wants to be a weed, no matter what you do, that person will be a weed. Spending all your time and energy trying to change them is going to keep you from blooming. One of the best things you can do is just bloom bigger than ever right in the middle of those weeds. Right in the middle of those negative and critical co-workers, put a big smile on your face.

Be kind. Be friendly. When they complain, don't preach a sermon to them. Don't try to stop them. Your job is not to pull up the weeds. Your job is to bloom. Just have a good report. The more they complain, the more grateful you should be. The more they talk defeat, the more you should talk victory.

If your co-workers come in one morning being sour and rude to you, don't be offended and think, *Well, I'm never going to speak to them again.* That's the time more than ever to bloom. Put a smile on your face anyway. Have a good attitude in spite of that.

If you spend all your time trying to encourage others, trying to make them do what's right, trying to keep them cheered up, they'll drain all the life and energy out of you. You cannot bloom if you spend all your time trying to keep others happy. That is not your responsibility.

I learned long ago that not everyone wants to be happy. Some people want to live in the pits. They like the attention it brings them. Make the decision to say: "If you don't want to be happy, that's fine, but you can't keep me from being happy. If you want to live in the pits, that's your choice, but I'm not diving in there with you. If you want to be a weed, you can be a weed, but I'm a flower. I'm blooming. I'm choosing a good attitude. I'm smiling. I'm happy despite my circumstances."

When you bloom in the midst of weeds, you sow a seed to inspire and challenge the people around you to come up higher, and that's a seed for God to take you higher.

You may be in a negative environment right now. The people in your life may not be going places. They may lack goals, dreams, vision, and enthusiasm. You may not see how you could ever rise above. It might be easy to just accept and settle where you are and think this is your destiny.

Let me challenge you. This is not your destiny. You were made for more. Your lot in life is to excel. It's to go further. It's to make a difference in this world. Take a stand and say, "I will not settle where I am. I was made for more. I'm a child of the Most High God. I have seeds of greatness on the inside. So I am rising up to be the best I can be right here, knowing God will take me where I'm supposed to go."

## Consider This

We are responsible for helping and encouraging others, for guiding them further along. But we are not responsible for their choices. You cannot force a good attitude upon someone. If they want to live in the pits, unhappy, discouraged, and in self-pity, that's their choice. Do not allow them to drag you into the pit with them.

_____

_____

_____

_____

_____

_____

_____

_____

Experience is by industry achieved and perfected by the swift course of time.

—William Shakespeare

_____

_____

_____

_____

_____

_____

_____

_____

_____

## What the Scriptures Say

Not that I was ever in need, for I have learned how to be content with whatever I have.

—Philippians 4:11 (NLT)

True godliness with contentment is itself great wealth.

—1 Timothy 6:6 (NLT)

## A Prayer for Today

Father, I trust You. I may not understand what's going on right now. I may not be comfortable, and I may not feel like following this path, but I'm doing it unto You.

_____

_____

_____

_____

_____

_____

_____

_____

_____

The years teach much which the days never know.

—Ralph Waldo Emerson

_____

_____

_____

_____

_____

_____

_____

_____

_____

_____

*Takeaway Truth*

God has incredible things planned for you
in your future. You have to do your part and
bloom where you're planted. Develop your gifts
and talents. Whatever you do, whatever your
occupation is, do your best to be the best.

## DAY 6

# *Slow Down and Enjoy the Journey*

* * * * * * * * * * * * * * * * * * * * * * * * * * * * * * * * * * * *

*Key Truth*

A joyful life isn't simply about big victories, it's
about finding happiness in each moment.

* * * * * * * * * * * * * * * * * * * * * * * * * * * * * * * * * * * *

Former football star Deion Sanders had a dream to win the Super
Bowl. That's what he wanted more than anything else. He trained
and trained, year after year, working tirelessly. One day his dream
came to pass. His team, the San Francisco 49ers, won the Super Bowl
after the 1994 season. After the big celebration, he was so disap-
pointed. *Is this all that it is?* he thought. *I've worked and reached the
pinnacle of my career. I thought it would be different. Yes, I'm happy.
Yes, God has blessed me. But it's just not what I thought it would be.*

Some spend their whole lives trying to reach a goal only to find
out it's not what it was all cracked up to be. My friend, the real joy is
in the simple things. It's in being with your family, getting up early
and seeing the sunrise, taking a walk through the park, taking your
daughter to lunch, going on a bike ride with your spouse. Of course,
the goals, and accomplishments, bring us a sense of satisfaction, but
they're only temporary.

You can't live off your big events because after you savor them for
a moment, God will birth a new dream in your heart, something new
to look forward to.

I've talked to many people who have made it to the very top in their fields. The one common regret I hear is that they succeeded, but at the expense of their families. They say, "If I could do it over again, I would take time to stop and smell the roses. I would be there for my children's Little League games. I wouldn't live so stressed and uptight, thinking, 'If I could just get to the next level, then I'll slow down and enjoy my life.'"

Slow down and enjoy the journey right now. Take time for the people God has put in your life. They won't always be there.

Every day, tell your spouse, your children, those who mean the most to you, how much you love them. I told Victoria the other day how much I appreciate her coming and listening to me speak every service. Awhile back we were out of town holding services. Then we returned to Lakewood Church and did three services on the weekend. And I figured she had heard my same message eight times in a row. Listen, after eight times, I'm even tired of it. But she sits there, three services every week, and she laughs at my same jokes each time, as though it's the first time she's heard them. I know she's faking it, but at least she's faking it to make me feel good.

I don't take that for granted. Make sure the people in your life know how much you appreciate their sacrificing and supporting you. After all, you wouldn't be where you are if somebody wasn't paying the price to help you move further down the road.

My mother is another great example of this support. Every service when I'm preaching I hear her egging me on from the front row. Under her breath she's constantly whispering, "That's good, Joel." It doesn't matter what I'm talking about. I'm her son. She thinks everything I say is great. Why, I can say to the congregation, "You may be seated," and my mom will say, "Oh, that's excellent today, Joel."

I wouldn't be where I am today without those who have sown into my life. I'll never take for granted those closest to me—my family, my friends, my co-workers—all of those making sacrifices so I can fulfill what God has put in my heart.

Many people these days are making a living, but they're not really making their lives. They're working all the time, living stressed-out, bringing the tension home, too busy to enjoy what God has given them. Understand that when you come to the end of your life, most likely there will still be work to do at the office. Your in-box will still be full. Your work will never be finished.

## Consider This

It's good to be focused and driven. It's good to be a hard worker. But it's important that you know how to put your work aside, walk away, and say, "You know what? This work is still going to be at the office tomorrow. So I'll do my best today. I'm working hard, but I'm also playing hard. I'm enjoying my family. I'm having fun with my children." If you don't make this decision, your family will have only your leftover time and leftover energy. They deserve better.

_____

_____

_____

_____

_____

_____

_____

_____

One should count each day a separate life.
—Lucius Annaeus Seneca

_____

_____

_____

---------------------------------------

---------------------------------------

---------------------------------------

---------------------------------------

---------------------------------------

---------------------------------------

## What the Scriptures Say

How do you know what your life will be like tomorrow? Your
life is like the morning fog—it's here a little while, then it's gone.

—James 4:14 (NLT)

We do not lose heart. Though outwardly we are wasting away,
yet inwardly we are being renewed day by day. For our light
and momentary troubles are achieving for us an eternal glory
that far outweighs them all. So we fix our eyes not on what is
seen, but on what is unseen, since what is seen is temporary, but
what is unseen is eternal.

—2 Corinthians 4:16–18 (NIV)

## A Prayer for Today

Father, help me trust in Your plans for me, and give me the wisdom
to enjoy the people You put in my life and place in my path.

---------------------------------------

---------------------------------------

---------------------------------------

---------------------------------------

---------------------------------------

---------------------------------------

_____

_____

_____

Today is life—the only life you are sure of. Make the most of today.

—Dale Carnegie

_____

_____

_____

_____

_____

_____

_____

### Takeaway Truth

If you don't make your family and those you love a high priority to enjoy, to spend time with, and to invest in, you will miss out on what matters most. In your final days here on this earth, the job won't keep you company. Your family will. But if you spend all your time just investing in a career, giving the best of your life and energy to build a business, then your lack of investment in what matters most—your family—could leave you a very lonely person.

# Some Things You Can't Get Back

*Key Truth*

Every day is about creating memories to last
a lifetime.

W hen our daughter, Alexandra, was about three years old, she used to wake up at night and come down the stairs into our room. Of course, we would have to take her back to bed. For a few months she was waking up two or three times a night and coming down.

This was not long after I took over for my father and started pastoring. I was learning to minister, and there was a lot of stress and change just with that, so I wasn't sleeping much. One time I was telling Victoria, "We've just got to do something about Alexandra. She's coming down so much. You know, I'm just so tired. I'm not getting enough sleep." On and on.

Victoria said something I'll never forget. She said, "Joel, just remember, twenty years from now, you'll give anything to hear those little footsteps coming down the stairs. You'll give anything to have her wanting to come into your room."

That changed my whole perspective. I began looking forward to it. I treasured those moments that we could spend together. Your children may be a lot of work right now, but make sure you're enjoying them. They won't always be in the house with you.

You have to realize that there are some things you cannot get back.

Your children will be home for only so long. Take time for the people in your life. Don't rush out of the house without giving your spouse a hug. Don't be so busy that you can't go on that promised date with your child. Don't come home so tired that you can't go to the park and watch your teenager skateboard.

Make memories together. Twenty years from now you will look back and say, "Those were the good old days. Remember when our baby woke us up every night? Remember when our child made the game-winning shot? Remember when I'd take you to the park and chase you around? Remember when we'd sit around the dinner table and laugh and tell stories?"

I heard someone say, "It's not the time we spend together. It's the moments we ignite to make memories."

I know plenty of people who live in a house full of family but who are very lonely. Everybody is busy. Everyone is doing his or her own thing. Nobody is stepping up to say, "You know what? We're a family. We take time to sit together at the dinner table and catch up. We enjoy the ball game or a dance recital and cheering on family members. We lift up one another when we're falling. We're enjoying what God has given us."

It's easy to be too busy. It's easy to become disengaged. But if you want the most out of life, draw the line and say, "I'm slowing down and enjoying the journey. I'm not taking for granted what God has given me. I'm not being a workaholic, and I'm not missing the years when my children are growing up. I'm not living so stressed out that I can't appreciate the simple things in life."

A few years ago I was rounding everybody up at our house to leave for church, and we were running late. I was in a big hurry, all stressed out. Our son, Jonathan, was about eight years old. Somebody had given us a label-maker, one of those little machines that prints out a label with a sticker on the back after you type in the desired text. Jonathan was by the back door typing something into the machine.

"Jonathan, put that up," I said. "We're late. We've got to go right now."

He said, "Hang on, Dad. I just need another minute, just another second."

I said, "Jonathan, we don't have another second. We're not going to get to church in time. You've got to put it up." I was getting more and more stressed out.

About that time he printed out the message and handed it to me.

"You're the best dad in the world," it said.

I thought, *Well, maybe we can stay here a little longer, and print out a few more of those.*

Sometimes we become so caught up in our goals and so focused on the end result that we miss the miracles all along the way. Take time to smell the roses. Enjoy the different personalities God has put in your life.

## Consider This

I've found it's the simple things that mean the most. You don't have to take an expensive vacation to make a memory. You can create a memory sitting at the dinner table. You can experience a memorable moment watching your children play in the backyard, or rising early with your spouse and taking in a beautiful sunrise.

_____

_____

_____

_____

_____

_____

_____

_____

_____

_____

Footfalls echo in the memory
Down the passage which we did not take
Towards the door we never opened.

—T. S. Eliot

_____

_____

_____

_____

_____

_____

_____

## What the Scriptures Say

I have told you all this so that you may have peace in me. Here on earth you will have many trials and sorrows. But take heart, because I have overcome the world.

—John 16:33 (NLT)

God is our refuge and strength, always ready to help in times of trouble. So we will not fear when earthquakes come and the mountains crumble into the sea. Let the oceans roar and foam. Let the mountains tremble as the waters surge!

—Psalm 46:1–3 (NLT)

## A Prayer for Today

Heavenly Father, thank You for breathing in my direction. Thank You for giving life to my dreams, hopes, and desires. I give You glory for every good thing in my life.

_____

_____

Nothing is worth more than this day.
                              —Johann Wolfgang von Goethe

### Takeaway Truth

You are living in tomorrow's good old days.
Don't take now for granted. Your family
needs what you have. They need your smile,
your encouragement, your support, and your
wisdom. They need to know you care and that
they mean the world to you. It's important
not to just be *in* the house. Don't just show
up. Be involved. Be engaged.

# STEP TWO

......................................

## *Know What to Ignore*

# DAY 1

## *Recognize Your Gifts*

. . . . . . . . . . . . . . . . . . . . . . . . . . . . . . . . . . . . . . .

*Key Truth*

Happiness comes when you focus not on what
you lack, but on your blessings.

. . . . . . . . . . . . . . . . . . . . . . . . . . . . . . . . . . . . . . . . .

A middle-aged man named Nicholas was very down and discouraged so he went to his minister.

"Nothing in my life is going right," he said. "I have no reason to be
excited, no reason to be thankful."

"All right, let's do a little exercise," the minister said.

He took out a legal pad and drew a line down the middle.

"Let's list all your assets on this side, all the things that are right
in your life," the minister said. "On the other side we'll list all your
challenges, all the things that are bothering you."

Nicholas laughed.

"I have nothing on my asset side," he said, hanging his head.

"That's fine, but let's just go through the exercise," said the minister, adding, "I'm so sorry to hear that your wife has passed away."

Nicholas looked up abruptly.

"What are you talking about? My wife didn't pass away. She's alive
and healthy."

The minister calmly said, "Oh," and then wrote down under
assets "Healthy wife."

Next the minister said, "Nicholas, I'm so sorry to hear your house burned down."

"My house didn't burn down," said Nicholas.

Again, the minister calmly said, "Oh," and added "Place to live" to the list of assets.

The minister was on a roll.

"Nicholas, I'm so sorry to hear that you were laid off from work."

"Pastor, where are you getting all this nonsense?" he said. "I have a good job."

The minister wrote "A good job" on the list of assets.

"Can I see that list?" Nicholas asked, finally catching on. After looking it over, he added a dozen more assets that he'd been taking for granted instead of being grateful for them. Nicholas left the minister's office with a much different attitude.

What was Nicholas's problem? He just needed to change his perspective. When he began to focus on the good in his life, he got his happiness and joy back.

You have to realize that every day is a gift from God. You are not always going to be here. What a shame to live this day or any other day defeated, depressed, negative, complaining, and with no enthusiasm. We all have obstacles. We all have things to overcome, but our attitude should be: *I know God is still on the throne. He's in complete control of my life. He's said His plans for me are for good and not evil. I'm not living this day defeated, depressed, or focused on what I don't have. I'm changing my perspective. Thank God I'm alive. Thank God I'm breathing. Thank God I'm healthy. Thank God for my family. I'm living every day to the fullest.*

Some people feel burdened by their duties and responsibilities, but those, too, are gifts. They complain because they "have to go to work" or they "have to take care of the kids." You don't *have* to do anything. You *get* to do all those things. God gives you breath. You couldn't go to work, take care of the kids, or mow the yard if God didn't give you the strength. You couldn't go to work if He didn't give you the opportunity.

Change your perspective. You don't *have* to go to work; you *get* to go to work. You don't *have* to take care of your children; you *get* to take care of your children.

Do you know how many people would give anything to have children? Some couples spend thousands of dollars and go through painful medical procedures in their efforts to have children. They would give anything to be cleaning up after their own kids. Thank God everyday for blessing you with children. They are a gift from God.

## Consider This

If you struggle with staying encouraged and staying grateful, make a list of everything God has blessed you with. If you have your health, write it down as an asset. If your vision is good, write it down, too. The same with your job, your family, your friends, your spouse, your children, and all your other blessings. Make that list and then go over it throughout the day. That should get you thinking in the right direction.

_____

_____

_____

_____

_____

_____

_____

I would maintain that thanks are the highest form of thought, and that gratitude is happiness doubled by wonder.
—Gilbert K. Chesterton

_____

_____

_____

_____

_____

_____

_____

_____

_____

## What the Scriptures Say

O give thanks to the Lord, for He is good; for His mercy and loving-kindness endure forever!

—1 Chronicles 16:34 (AMP)

In the morning, LORD, you hear my voice; in the morning I lay my requests before you and wait expectantly.

—Psalm 5:3 (NIV)

## A Prayer for Today

Father in heaven, today I declare my thanks to You for all You have done in my life. Help me see Your hand of blessing as I continually acknowledge and praise Your name. Fill me with Your peace and joy as I keep You first place in all that I do. In Jesus' name. Amen.

_____

_____

_____

_____

_____

_____

_____

Joy is the simplest form of gratitude.

—Karl Barth

_____

_____

_____

_____

_____

_____

_____

. . . . . . . . . . . . . . . . . . . . . . . . . . . . . . . . . . . . . . . . . . . . . . .

### Takeaway Truth

If you're to have the right perspective, you
need to appreciate the simple things God
has blessed you with.

. . . . . . . . . . . . . . . . . . . . . . . . . . . . . . . . . . . . . . . . . . . . . . .

# DAY 2

## *Stay on the High Road*

*Key Truth*

Whatever your critics say about you has no
bearing on your worth. You are a child of
the Most High God.

Not long ago, a reporter asked me what I thought about two men he named. I said I didn't know who they were and I had never heard of them. The reporter laughed and laughed. He thought that was so funny.

"Well, who are they?" I asked.

"They are your two most outspoken critics," he said. "They're always talking about you."

He couldn't believe that I had never heard of them. But I've learned this principle: I don't waste time engaging in conflicts that don't matter to me. I've learned that the critics cannot keep me from my destiny. What they say about me doesn't define who I am.

The Creator of the universe breathed life into you. You have seeds of greatness on the inside. You've been crowned with favor. God has already equipped and empowered you with everything you need. Don't waste your valuable time trying to play up to people, trying to win over all your critics, or trying to prove to someone that you're important.

Accept the fact that some people are never going to celebrate you. They will never recognize your gifts. That's okay. Don't be distracted. God has already lined up the right people to celebrate you, the right people who will cheer you on and help you fulfill your destiny.

If you want to live in victory, you have to be very careful with your time and attention. You have to know what thoughts to ignore, what comments to ignore, and, I say this respectfully, what people to ignore.

If someone at work is always on your nerves, making sarcastic comments, you could try to straighten them out, but you'd be wasting valuable time and energy that could be spent pursuing your dreams. Don't be distracted. Ignore such people.

If a family member never gives you any credit, either you can let that upset and frustrate you or you can dismiss it and say, "No big deal. I don't need their approval. I have almighty God's approval."

You don't have to straighten people out. You don't have to pay somebody back. You don't have to be offended because of what someone said. You can ignore it and live happily. I'm convinced we would enjoy life a whole lot more if we would get good at knowing what to ignore.

According to Mark 3:1-5, Jesus was in the temple on a Sabbath, the day of rest, when He saw a man with a withered hand. Jesus simply said, "Stretch out your hand" (v. 5 NIV), and immediately the man was healed. The religious leaders, the Pharisees, were there and they didn't like Jesus. They didn't understand Him. They got together and said, "Yes, Jesus did do something good. He did heal a man. But you know what? He did it on the wrong day. He shouldn't have been working on the Sabbath."

## Consider This

Some will condemn you no matter what you do. Even if you changed and did everything they asked of you, they would still find fault. Let me pass on a secret to save you heartache and pain: Ignore your critics. You don't need their approval. You don't need their approval or their disapproval. Stay on the high road. The more they talk, the more God will bless you. They may try to take you down. God will take you up.

---
---
---
---
---
---
---
---

> Any fool can criticize, condemn and complain and most fools do.
> —Benjamin Franklin

---
---
---
---
---
---
---
---
---

## What the Scriptures Say

Always be humble and gentle. Be patient with each other, making allowance for each other's faults because of your love.
—Ephesians 4:2 (NLT)

Do not judge others, and you will not be judged. Do not condemn others, or it will all come back against you. Forgive others, and you will be forgiven.

—Luke 6:37 (NLT)

## A Prayer for Today

Father, thank You for another day to see Your goodness in my life. Help me to see myself the way You see me. Help me to see the plans You have for me so that I can be empowered by You to fulfill my destiny. I love You and bless Your name today.

_____

_____

_____

_____

_____

_____

_____

_____

_____

The strength of criticism lies only in the weakness of the thing criticized.

—Henry Wadsworth Longfellow

_____

_____

_____

_____

_____

_____

_____

_____

_____

. . . . . . . . . . . . . . . . . . . . . . . . . . . . . . . . . . . . . . . . . .

### *Takeaway Truth*

You will rise higher by ignoring your critics
and focusing on God's best in you.

. . . . . . . . . . . . . . . . . . . . . . . . . . . . . . . . . . . . . . . . . .

## DAY 3

## *Choose Your Battles Wisely*

*Key Truth*

Many of the challenges that may come your way
are simply distractions meant to lure you from
your destiny.

In the early years of our marriage, I had a pet peeve. If Victoria didn't turn off all the lights when she left the house, I'd get uptight.

"Victoria, be sure to turn off all the lights!"

A few hours later, I'd come home to an empty house with all the lights on. I would tell her once again we were paying too much on our power bills.

I knew she didn't leave the lights on intentionally. She just left without thinking to turn them off because she had other things on her mind. I'm more of a details person. Victoria is more of a big-picture person. We just have different personalities and different strengths.

I harped at her for about five years before I put that pet peeve down.

After all that time of bringing tension into the house, getting uptight, it finally dawned on me, *Joel, this is not a battle worth fighting. If it costs you an extra ten dollars a month in electricity, it's well worth keeping the peace in your home.*

The lower power bills were not worth the higher stress and heartache. Learn from my mistake. How much tension are you bringing into the home unnecessarily? You may win a victory, but will it be worth the stress?

Have you ever heard the saying "A bulldog can whip a skunk any day of the week. But sometimes even a dog realizes it's just not worth the stink"?

Winning isn't everything.

Peace on the home front and a loving relationship are worth a few nicks in the ego. I've found it's easy to start a fight, but it's hard to end one. The best strategy is to take a step back, draw a deep breath, and say, "What truly matters here?"

If you want God to honor you, if you want to enjoy your life, be a peacemaker. Be the kind of person who avoids an unnecessary fight, a fight that carries no real rewards.

Your home needs to be a place of peace. You and your spouse need to be in harmony. You are stronger together than you are apart. Not only that, your children need to see a good example. They will treat their own spouses the same way they've seen their parents treat each other.

Fight mode should not be your daily setting. You likely have friends, family members, or coworkers who constantly run hot. They are always aggravated at a spouse, a neighbor, or someone in the office. Anger consumes their time and energy. They don't know when a battle is not worth fighting because there are no spoils. Even if they win, they'll be no further down the road toward happiness or fulfillment.

## Consider This

If you make the mistake of engaging in every potential battle that comes along, and you are constantly defending yourself, proving your point, straightening out others, then you probably won't have the energy to fight the battles that do matter. Even a warrior knows when to sit one out. He saves his energy for the battles that mean something; those that move him closer to his God-given destiny.

_____

_____

_____

_____

_____

_____

_____

We are not at peace with others because we are not at peace
with ourselves, and we are not at peace with ourselves because
we are not at peace with God.

—Thomas Merton

_____

_____

_____

_____

_____

_____

_____

## What the Scriptures Say

Avoiding a fight is a mark of honor; only fools insist on quar-
reling.

—Proverbs 20:3 (NLT)

Do you not know that in a race all the runners compete, but
[only] one receives the prize? So run [your race] that you may
lay hold [of the prize] and make it yours.

—1 Corinthians 9:24 (AMP)

## A Prayer for Today

Father, today I choose to refocus on You. I am determined to overlook offenses and choose my battles wisely. I will run the race You have set before me with purpose so I can lay hold of the prize You have for me.

_____

_____

_____

_____

_____

_____

_____

_____

Have you heard that it was good to gain the day? I also say it is good to fall, battles are lost in the same spirit in which they are won.

—Walt Whitman

_____

_____

_____

_____

_____

_____

_____

_____

_____

### Takeaway Truth

You may miss out on God's best while distracted by battles that don't matter. Maybe you are trying to prove your worth, trying to win over your critics, or playing for approval. Those are all needless distractions. Choose your battles wisely.

# DAY 4

## *Focus on the Good*

*Key Truth*

You can't do anything about your past, but you
can do something about your future.

Three men were carrying two sacks each. A passerby asked the first man what was in the sacks.

"The sack on my back is filled with all the good things that have happened to me," he said. "The sack in the front is filled with all the bad."

He was constantly focused on the bad things in front of him so he couldn't even see the good on his back.

The stranger asked the second man the same question but received the opposite response.

"The sack in the back is filled with the bad things," he said. "The sack in the front is filled with the good things."

At least he could see the good and not focus on the negative. But both of the sacks being so full still weighed him down and made life a burden.

Finally, the stranger asked the third man the same question.

"The sack on my chest is filled with my accomplishments and victories," he said. "The sack on my back is empty."

"Why is it empty?" the stranger asked.

"I put all my mistakes, failures, guilt and shame in that sack, and

I cut a hole in the bottom to release them," he said. "That way, I'm weighted in the front more than the back so I keep moving forward. In fact, the empty sack in the back acts like a sail in the wind, moving me ahead."

Like that third man, you have to let go of the bad, hang on to the good, and keep moving forward toward your goals.

One way you know that guilt and condemnation are not from God is that they don't help you improve. Guilt and condemnation don't make you do better. When you go around feeling bad about yourself, you are much more likely to make another mistake. I've seen people on diets despair so much they need a bowl of ice cream to recover. They give up on their goals because guilt doesn't make them do better; it makes them do worse.

The correct way to handle guilt is to repent and ask for forgiveness. Move forward. The wrong way is to hold on to guilt for a week, a year, or a lifetime. There are some things you cannot undo. You can't unscramble eggs. You cannot relive yesterday, but you can live today. Don't let the accuser sour your future any longer. Start dwelling on what's right with you, not what's wrong with you.

Have you noticed how human nature is drawn toward the negative? I can have a hundred people tell me after a service, "That was a great message. I really needed to hear that." But then one person will say, "I don't know if I really understood the point. I'm not really sure I agree with you on that."

I used to go home depressed, discouraged, feeling like a failure. I've learned now to shake it off. If somebody doesn't like my message, my attitude is: *You have every right to disagree with me, but I'm not going to let that make me feel inadequate.* I will not allow one bad report to cancel out a hundred good reports. In the same way, don't let one weakness or one mistake made cancel out all the other great things about you. You may have made a lot of wrong choices, but you've also made a lot of choices that were right.

Focus on your good qualities. Focus on your victories. Get off the treadmill of guilt. It's not taking you anywhere. Guilt will steal your joy. Don't live another moment in regret. The source of your guilt may have been your fault, but that's what mercy is all about. Rise up and say, "This is a new day. I'm unloading the baggage. I am done feeling wrong about myself. I'm done feeling condemned. I've focused long enough on what I've done wrong. I'm focusing on what I'm doing right."

## Consider This

It's very difficult for most people to accept the fact that God forgives us so easily. When we make mistakes, we think we have to pay for them. So we grow discouraged and get down on ourselves. Sure, we should be remorseful when we do wrong. We should be genuinely sorry and not flippant. But you don't have to spend month after month wallowing around in guilt and condemnation. Move on.

_____

_____

_____

_____

_____

_____

_____

_____

Forgiveness is the key which unlocks the door of resentment and the handcuffs of hatred. It breaks the chains of bitterness and the shackles of selfishness.

—Corrie ten Boom

_____

_____

_____

_____

_____

_____

_____

_____

_____

## What the Scriptures Say

Mercy triumphs over judgment.

—James 2:13 (NIV)

"'This is what you are to say to Joseph: I ask you to forgive your brothers the sins and the wrongs they committed in treating you so badly.' Now please forgive the sins of the servants of the God of your father." When their message came to him, Joseph wept.

—Genesis 50:16–17 (NIV)

## A Prayer for Today

Father, thank You for Your mercy. Thank You for receiving me, loving me, cleansing me, and changing me. I dedicate every area of my life to You and invite You to have Your way in me.

_____

_____

_____

_____

_____

_____

Life is an adventure in forgiveness.

—Norman Cousins

_____

_____

_____

_____

_____

_____

_____

_____

_____

*Takeaway Truth*

Do not spend time thinking about what's wrong
with you. Focus instead on what's right with
you and build upon it.

# Turn Your Disadvantages into Advantages

*Key Truth*
God knows how to take what should be a disadvantage and turn it into an advantage.

I am a sports fan. I love the classic and true story of a boy whose dream was to play professional baseball. He was extremely gifted. All through junior high and high school he was by far the most talented player in his league. Professional scouts were regularly at his games.

Then one day he had a farming accident. He lost the whole forefinger and most of the middle finger on his throwing hand. It looked like his baseball days were over. But this young man had a "no-excuses" mentality. He learned to throw the ball without those two fingers, even though they are usually the main fingers used to throw a baseball.

He had always been a third baseman, but one afternoon during practice the coach was standing behind this young man and noticed some interesting movement on the ball when he threw from third to first. The coach asked him to try pitching. Turns out that was a very good idea.

Mordecai "Three Finger" Brown went on to become one of the greatest pitchers in the early history of Major League Baseball. In fact, he played for six different teams including the St. Louis Cardinals and the Chicago Cubs, competing until the age of forty. He helped win two World Series and was inducted into the Baseball Hall of Fame in 1949.

What many thought would be a liability turned out to be a great asset. The spin Three Finger Brown could put on the ball made it very difficult to hit. God knows how to take what should be a disadvantage and turn it into an advantage.

It's often easy to come up with explanations as to why you can't do or be your best. Most people think they have a handicap of one kind or another, something that is holding them back. It may be a physical challenge, a personality issue, or maybe a divorce or a financial problem.

I've heard many explanations including "I'm just the wrong nationality." And "I was born on the wrong side of the tracks." If you find yourself apologizing for being different, why not start looking at yourself as unique instead? You are not too tall or too short. You are just the right size. You have just the right personality, just the right looks, and just the right talents.

When God made you He wasn't having a bad day. He made you to be the way you are on purpose. He finished creating you and then He stepped back and said, "That was good. I like that; another masterpiece." There may be things about you that you don't like, but you can't allow those things to hold you back or keep you from pursuing your dreams.

## Consider This

We all have things that can feel like disadvantages, things that make life harder on us. But just because you have a "disadvantage," just because you've been through a tough time, doesn't mean you should sit back and settle where you are. No, God still has something great for you to do! He wants to show Himself strong in and through you. The Holy Spirit wants to help you during those times when you feel weak. If you will stay in faith and not get negative toward yourself or your future, then God can take what you think is a liability and turn it into an asset. What you think is a disadvantage, God will turn around to be an advantage so you can move forward into the abundant life He has for you!

_____

_____

_____

_____

_____

_____

_____

_____

We gain strength, and courage, and confidence by each experience in which we really stop to look fear in the face...we must do that which we think we cannot.

—Eleanor Roosevelt

_____

_____

_____

_____

_____

_____

_____

_____

## What the Scriptures Say

And the Holy Spirit helps us in our weakness....

—Romans 8:26 (NLT)

He said to me, "My grace is sufficient for you, for my power is made perfect in weakness." Therefore I will boast all the more gladly about my weaknesses, so that Christ's power may rest on me.

—2 Corinthians 12:9 (NIV)

## A Prayer for Today

Father in heaven, today I give You all that I am. I invite You into the weak places in my life so that You can turn them into strengths. Thank You for working in my life and filling me with faith and expectancy.

_____

_____

_____

_____

_____

_____

_____

_____

We acquire the strength we have overcome.

—Ralph Waldo Emerson

_____

_____

_____

_____

_____

_____

_____

_____

*Takeaway Truth*

Each of us has challenges to overcome, but just because you think you have a "disadvantage," doesn't mean you should sit back and settle where you are. God still has something great for you to do. You may not look like everyone else. You may not be able to do what some others can do. But if you will stay in faith and stay positive about your future, you can turn your liabilities into assets.

# DAY 6

## *Trust God's Plan*

*Key Truth*
You must take what God gives you and
make the very most of it.

I have another minister friend by the name of David Ring. Like my sister Lisa, he was born with a form of cerebral palsy. But God's plan for his life was different. Lisa miraculously recovered from her childhood illness. David Ring was not healed. When he talks it takes him three or four times as long as most people to get the words out. When he walks, his legs and arms don't function normally.

David easily could have sat at home and thought, *Too bad for me. I have this disability. My speech is slow. I can't get around. God, I thought You wanted me to do something great. I thought You wanted me to be a minister. I must have been wrong. I have this handicap.*

Let me tell you about David Ring: Nothing slows him down. He travels the world speaking to thousands of people, telling them about the goodness of God and encouraging them to overcome obstacles. When he speaks, he is difficult to understand because he speaks very slowly. But I love the way he always starts. He says, "My name is David Ring. What's your excuse?"

Think about this. Lisa was healed from cerebral palsy, and she's honoring God with her life. David Ring is living with cerebral palsy, and he's honoring God with his life. What am I saying? You must take what God gives you and make the very most of it. You cannot sit around thinking, *Why did this happen to me?*

God could have healed David just like He restored my sister Lisa. But God is sovereign. I don't claim to understand it all, but I do know this: God is good. He has a great plan for your life, a destiny for you to fulfill. No matter how many disadvantages or setbacks you must deal with, if you shake off the self-pity, stop blaming, and keep pressing forward, nothing will be able to keep you from becoming all that God created you to be.

Stop making excuses. Quit dwelling on disappointments, on the unfairness and hurt inflicted upon you. Know that God has something great coming your way. The worst handicaps are those you place on yourself. Too many people are waiting for God to make them perfect before they pursue their dreams and destinies. Go after yours right now.

Honor God with what you have. He wants to take your liabilities and turn them into assets. First, though, you have to accept that God may not remove your challenge, but He will use it to your advantage.

In the Scripture there is a story of a man who was born blind (see John 9). Some people were asking Jesus, "Why was he born this way?" and "Whose fault was it, his or his parents?"

They were trying to find someone to blame, a reason or an excuse. We tend to do the same things today. But I love the way Jesus answered. He said, "It's not anybody's fault, not his or his parents. The reason he was born this way was so that the goodness of God could be displayed."

Jesus was saying when you have a setback, or when life deals you a tough blow, don't be bitter. Don't settle there. Recognize that you are a prime candidate for God to show His favor and goodness through.

## Consider This

If you feel you are disadvantaged or disabled, instead of saying, "It's not fair, God," your attitude should be: *God, I'm ready. I know You have something great in store. I refuse to live defeated and depressed. I know this disadvantage is simply another opportunity for You to show up and show out.*

_____

_____

_____

_____

_____

_____

_____

_____

_____

It has been my philosophy of life that difficulties vanish when faced boldly.

—Isaac Asimov

_____

_____

_____

_____

_____

_____

_____

_____

## What the Scriptures Say

"It was not because of his sins or his parents' sins," Jesus answered. "This happened so the power of God could be seen in him."

—John 9:3 (NLT)

As the heavens are higher than the earth, so are my ways higher than your ways and my thoughts than your thoughts.

—Isaiah 55:9 (NIV)

## A Prayer for Today

Father, today I choose to trust in You. I trust that You are working behind the scenes on my behalf. I release all of my cares and concerns to You, knowing that You have a greater plan in store for me.

_____

_____

_____

_____

_____

_____

_____

Faith is to believe what you do not yet see; the reward for this faith is to see what you believe.

—Saint Augustine

_____

_____

_____

_____

_____

_____

_____

_____

_____

_____

*Takeaway Truth*

Faith is all about trusting God, even when
you don't understand His plan.

## DAY 7

# God Will Be Your Vindicator

*Key Truth*

As your vindicator, God will bring justice,
and He will promote you.

A mechanic at a big diesel shop told me that for many years he was treated unfairly at work. It was a very negative environment. His co-workers constantly made fun of him. They thought he was a stiff because he wouldn't party with them after work. Year after year he had to endure this ridicule.

He was one of the best mechanics at that company, but in seven years he had never had a promotion, not a raise, or a bonus— nothing—because his supervisor didn't like him. He could have worked with a chip on his shoulder, but he took the high road, knowing God was his vindicator.

Then, one day, the owner of the company called him. They had never met because the owner wasn't involved in the day-to-day operations. But for some reason he called the mechanic and said he was retiring. He offered to sell his business to the mechanic.

"I don't have money to buy your company," the mechanic said.

"You don't need money," the owner said. "I will loan it to you."

Today, the mechanic owns the company free and clear. God set the table, and he was served. Now those who had called him names must call him Boss instead. They used to look down on him. Now they look up to him. They used to blow him off and not give him the time of day. Now they have to make an appointment if they want to see him!

## Consider This

The Bible says that faith comes by hearing the Word of God. You have to have faith in order to activate God's promises. When difficulties come and you're tempted to get upset, remind yourself, *This is not going to prosper against me. They may be talking about me. It may look bad. But I know God is my Vindicator. He'll take care of me. I know God has me in the palm of His hand.*

_____

_____

_____

_____

_____

_____

_____

_____

Problems are only opportunities in work clothes.

—Henry J. Kaiser

_____

_____

_____

_____

_____

_____

_____

_____

## What the Scriptures Say

When people's lives please the LORD, even their enemies are at peace with them.

—Proverbs 16:7 (NLT)

Keep this Book of the Law always on your lips; meditate on it day and night, so that you may be careful to do everything written in it. Then you will be prosperous and successful.

—Joshua 1:8 (NIV)

## A Prayer for Today

Father, thank You for every one of Your precious promises. Today I choose to meditate on Your Word, which brings life to my soul. Fill me with Your peace as I stand in faith until I see the victory You have in store for me.

_____

_____

_____

_____

_____

_____

_____

Comfort and prosperity have never enriched the world as much as adversity has.

—Billy Graham

_____

_____

_____

_____

_____

_____

_____

_____

_____

### Takeaway Truth

When you remind yourself of His promises, you
don't have to get worried. You know God is still
on the throne. You know that problem didn't
come to stay; it came to pass. So today, remind
yourself of His promises and feed your faith,
so that you can move forward in the victory
He has prepared for you!

# STEP THREE

## *Live Without Crutches*

# DAY 1

## Clear Out the Wrong to Get the Right

*Key Truth*

God will always bring the right people into your
life, but you have to let the wrong people walk
away. The right people will never show up if
you don't clear out the wrong.

Years ago there was a bright young lady who moved from a small town to work for our ministry. (I'll call her Diana here, but that's not her real name.) I noticed she always had a young man drop her off for work. One day, I asked her if she didn't have a car.

"Oh, I have a car," she said. "I drove everywhere in my small town. But when I moved here, my friend told me the city is so big and so complicated to drive in and since I'm not used to driving on the freeways, he would have to bring me to work every day."

I asked Diana if she ever planned to get behind the wheel herself, and she said probably not because her friend told her traffic is just so congested and difficult.

She was using this man as a crutch, and it appeared he might be manipulating her, controlling her for some reason, so I felt I had to say something.

"Diana, you are extremely talented," I said. "Do not allow any-one to convince you that you cannot drive on our freeways. I know eighteen-year-olds who are not as smart and bright as you who drive every day in this city without problems."

Diana shared with her friend what I'd said, and he still insisted that the streets were too dangerous for her and that she would get lost.

I told Diana that it seemed this young man was trying to make her dependent on him and that if he was a true friend, he would teach her how to get around so she could build up confidence enough to drive alone.

About a month later Diana told me that she'd driven to work on her own for the first time.

"That's great. I knew you could do it!" I said.

Then I asked how it had been to drive on the freeways.

"Oh, I don't drive on them," she said. "I take the side streets."

It should have taken Diana a half hour to drive to work. Instead it took her an hour. I encouraged her to keep driving and to work her way up to the freeways.

A month later she did it. Now Diana drives all over the city, and, isn't it interesting that the young man she was leaning on is no longer around?

He was interested in Diana only if he could keep her dependent on him and feeling that she owed him something. People like that are not true friends. They are not helping you. They are hindering you. You don't need people in your life who try to limit you. Let them go, and God will bring you the right people.

## Consider This

You don't need your friend to speak for you. You don't need your neighbor to drive for you. You don't need anyone to tell you what to do. You are equipped. God wouldn't have presented you with opportunities if He had not already given you everything you needed to take advantage of them.

_____

_____

_____

_____

_____

_____


Some things have to be believed to be seen.

—Ralph Hodgson

_____

_____

_____

_____

_____

_____

_____


## What the Scriptures Say

After this presentation to Israel's leaders, Moses and Aaron went and spoke to Pharaoh. They told him, "This is what the LORD, the God of Israel, says: Let my people go so they may hold a festival in my honor in the wilderness."

"Is that so?" retorted Pharaoh. "And who is the LORD? Why should I listen to him and let Israel go? I don't know the LORD, and I will not let Israel go."

But Aaron and Moses persisted. "The God of the Hebrews has met with us," they declared. "So let us take a three-day journey into the wilderness so we can offer sacrifices to the LORD our God. If we don't, he will kill us with a plague or with the sword."

Pharaoh replied, "Moses and Aaron, why are you distracting the people from their tasks? Get back to work!"

—Exodus 5:1–4 (NLT)

These people left our churches, but they never really belonged with us; otherwise they would have stayed with us. When they left, it proved that they did not belong with us.

—1 John 2:19 (NLT)

## A Prayer for Today

Father in Heaven, today I choose to put my hope in You. I know You have good plans for me. Thank You for renewing my strength and keeping me close to You. Fill me with Your peace and joy today.

_____

_____

_____

_____

_____

_____

_____

Your time is limited, so don't waste it living someone else's life. Don't be trapped by dogma—which is living with the results of other people's thinking. Don't let the noise of others' opinions drown out your own inner voice. And most importantly, have the courage to follow your heart and intuition. They somehow already know what you truly want to become. Everything else is secondary.

—Steve Jobs

_____

_____

_____

_____

_____

_____

_____

_____

_____

### Takeaway Truth

It's good to hear other people's opinions. It's
good to listen to advice. But understand that you
can also receive input from God. You can hear
that *still, small voice* from His Holy Spirit. You
have a direct line to the throne of God. And if
somebody is always trying to tell you what to
do, just say, "Thanks, but no thanks. God and I
are on speaking terms."

# DAY 2

## *Seek God's Approval*

*Key Truth*
To fulfill your destiny, stay
true to your heart.

When my father went to be with the Lord and I stepped up to pastor the church, an older gentleman I had known my whole life took me aside and said, "If this is going to work, here's what you're going to have to do."

He told me how to run the church, how to minister, how to lead the staff, how to move forward. I listened to his advice. I was very open. But nothing he said matched what I felt on the inside.

I prayed. I searched my own heart about what he'd told me, but nothing bore witness. I risked falling out of his good graces by following my own heart. The decision was difficult, but I went for God's approval, not this man's.

I stepped out and followed my heart, and God blessed my decision. The church thrived. I did fall out of the man's good graces, however. He wasn't happy that I did not take his advice.

Those who become upset if you don't do things their way are not really for you. They don't have your best interests at heart. If they were for you, they would be mature enough to say, "Even if you don't do it my way, even if you don't take my suggestions, I'll support you. I'll be behind you because I'm your friend and I want to see you succeed."

That's a true friend.

When I didn't take this man's advice, he was no longer on my side. It wasn't something big and obvious, just subtle things. I'd walk into a room and I could feel his sense of disapproval.

Thank God I didn't need his approval. He wasn't God. He wasn't sitting on the throne. He didn't write the plan for my life.

I looked to God instead and said, "He may not be for me, but I know You are for me. God, I may not have his approval, but I know I have Your approval. That's all that really matters."

I pressed forward doing what God put in my heart to do. God not only brought our church through that transition, but He brought us through bigger and better and greater than we ever had been. God knows what He is doing.

God will always give you direction for your life. Other people may have suggestions. They may have ideas. But God speaks directly to you. The Holy Spirit lives inside you. He leads you. He guides you.

Yes, be open and listen to your parents and mentors and friends, but follow your own heart. There is a still, small voice; a knowing inside you—that is God talking to you.

Be careful, though, about those who always have a word from the Lord to share with you. I grew up in church. I've heard a lot of words from the Lord, some of them right on, some of them way off. But anytime someone gives you a "word from the Lord," it should simply confirm what you already know on the inside.

When that older man told me how to run the church, his words didn't agree with anything that I was feeling. They were totally foreign. I've learned that God will not tell others what He wants for my life without telling me Himself. God and I are on speaking terms. We talk every single day.

If I would have been a people pleaser and run the church like that man wanted and ministered like he told me, I wouldn't be where I am today. I would have his approval, but what good would that do me?

I would rather have the approval of the Creator of the universe. I would rather have the God who spoke the worlds into existence smiling down on me.

## Consider This

To please God, you may have to displease people. This was a difficult concept for me because I want to please everybody. I want to be liked. When you follow what's in your heart, though, some may be unhappy with you. They may not understand. You may fall out of their favor. You may even lose friends.

_____

_____

_____

_____

_____

_____

_____

God is more interested in your future and your relationships than you are.

—Billy Graham

_____

_____

_____

_____

_____

_____

_____

_____

## What the Scriptures Say

The master was full of praise. "Well done, my good and faithful servant. You have been faithful in handling this small amount, so now I will give you many more responsibilities. Let's celebrate together!"

—Matthew 25:21 (NLT)

Before I formed you in the womb I knew and approved of you.

—Jeremiah 1:5 (AMP)

## A Prayer for Today

Heavenly Father, thank You for approving me and empowering me by Your love. I open my heart and mind to Your truth and invite You to have Your way in my life. Remove anything that would hold me back from all You have in store.

_____

_____

_____

_____

_____

_____

_____

_____

_____

To seek approval is to have no resting place, no sanctuary. Like all judgment, approval encourages a constant striving. It makes us uncertain of who we are and of our true value. Approval cannot be trusted. It can be withdrawn at any time no matter what our track record has been. It is as nourishing of real growth as cotton candy. Yet many of us spend our lives pursuing it.

—Rachel Naomi Remen

_____

_____

_____

_____

_____

_____

_____

_____

_____

### Takeaway Truth

Before you were born, God stamped His approval on you. You don't need to buy the friendship of anyone else. If you start a friendship off by buying it, you'll have to continue paying to keep it going. When you grow tired of doing what the person wants you to do, the friendship will end. They'll cut you loose. You are better off trusting God to bring you divine connections.

# DAY 3

## *Focus on Your Own Journey*

*Key Truth*
Accepting that you are not in competition will
free you to be God's best you.

I was out jogging one day and I noticed a person in front of me about a quarter of a mile. I could tell he was running a little slower than me and I thought, *Good. I'll try to catch him.*

I had about a mile to go on my path before I needed to turn off. So I started running faster and faster. Every block, I was gaining on him just a little bit. After just a few minutes I was only about 100 yards behind him, so I really picked up the pace and pushed myself. You would have thought I was running in the last leg of an Olympic competition. I was determined to catch him.

Finally, I did it. I caught and passed him by. On the inside I felt so good. *I beat him!* Of course, he didn't even know we were racing. After I passed him, I realized I'd been so focused on competing against him that I'd missed my turn.

I had gone nearly six blocks past it. I had to turn around and go all the way back.

Isn't that what happens in life when we focus on competing with our co-workers, or our neighbors, trying to outdo them or trying to prove that we are more successful or more important? We spend our time and energy running after them, and we miss out on our own paths to our God-given destinies.

Many of us would see our lives reach higher levels if we would quit competing with everyone around us and focus on our own races to be the best at what God made us to be. It takes a lot of energy, physical and emotional, to constantly be in competition with our neighbors, co-workers, or family members.

When you let go of that need to compete, it's very freeing. Tell yourself, *I don't have to impress anybody today. I have nothing to prove. I'm secure in who I am. I don't have to keep up with anyone. I'm not in that race.*

The problem with unhealthy competition is that it's a never-ending cycle. There will always be somebody ahead of you; someone with a better job, a bigger circle of friends, a nicer car, or more money in the bank. It's a very freeing thing when you realize you are not in a competition with your neighbors, friends, or co-workers. The only person you are competing with is yourself.

I realize I may not be the best minister in the world. I'm okay with that. But I'm dedicated to being the best minister I can be. I may not be as good a father as some other men, but that's okay. I'm not competing with anyone. I'm trying to be the best father I can be. I may not be the ideal husband. (Don't say, "Amen," Victoria.) But I'm working to be the best husband I can be.

Some people are insecure because they pay too much attention to what others are doing, where they are going, what they are wearing or driving. Instead, they should stay focused on their own goals. You're not anointed to compete with others. God gave you the grace to be who He has called you to be.

Confident, happy, and secure people stand out because what's on the inside shows on the outside. They are so comfortable in their own skins they're not easily intimidated. They don't feel inferior if they don't wear the best fashions or have the perfect physiques. They understand they're not in a competition. They're focused on being the best that they can be.

Take what God has given you, the height, the weight, the personality, and make the most of it. Dress it up and wear it proudly. I see too many people constantly frustrated and down about their looks, their height or weight. They're always fighting to fix what they don't like about themselves instead of accepting themselves.

## Consider This

When you have unhealthy competitive feelings, life is a constant struggle. You will never be good enough, because as soon as you catch up to one person, you'll find another ahead of you. That's not the way to find happiness in your everyday life, is it?

_____

_____

_____

_____

_____

_____

_____

To be nobody but yourself in a world that's doing its best to make you somebody else, is to fight the hardest battle you are ever going to fight. Never stop fighting.

—E. E. Cummings

_____

_____

_____

_____

_____

_____

_____

_____

_____

## What the Scriptures Say

I have observed something else under the sun. The fastest runner doesn't always win the race, and the strongest warrior doesn't always win the battle. The wise sometimes go hungry, and the skillful are not necessarily wealthy. And those who are educated don't always lead successful lives. It is all decided by chance, by being in the right place at the right time.

—Ecclesiastes 9:11 (NLT)

A heart at peace gives life to the body, but envy rots the bones.

—Proverbs 14:30 (NIV)

## A Prayer for Today

Father, thank You for Your Word, which is life to my soul. I praise You because You are the Prince of Peace and give peace to my heart and mind. I choose to stay focused on You today. Thank You for guiding my every step.

_____

_____

_____

_____

_____

_____

_____

_____

Insist upon yourself. Be original.

—Ralph Waldo Emerson

_____

_____

_____

_____

_____

_____

_____

### Takeaway Truth

Know that the "Best Possible You" may not be as
successful as your neighbor, but that's okay. The
best you may not be as thin as your sister, but
that's fine. The best you may not be as talented,
as dynamic, or as outgoing as your co-worker,
but that's all right, too. Be comfortable with
the person God made you to be. You can't get
distracted and lose your focus by comparing
yourself to others. Run your own race.

# DAY 4

## *Be Glad in Who You Are*

*Key Truth*
Happiness lies in accepting
who God made you to be.

In the New Testament, John was baptizing hundreds of people and making a name for himself when someone asked him: "Who are you?" (John 1:19 NKJV).

John knew what they were really asking, and without missing a beat, he said, "I am not the Christ" (v. 20 NKJV).

John knew what he was, and he also knew what he was not. It's just as important to know what you're not because if you don't realize your limitations, you may be drawn away from what God anointed you to do. Then you will be in a constant struggle.

Pride and competition can make it hard sometimes to admit what you are not. It takes a secure person to say, "I'm not gifted in that area, but I have my own talents."

When I hear our Spanish pastor, Marcos Witt, preach and then burst into song at the end of his sermon, I'm in awe of him. Of course, he is a musical person. He's won several Grammys, but he makes it seem effortless when he sings. I heard him the other day, and his singing gave me chill bumps up and down my arms.

My first thought was, *God, that's not fair. How come he's got two good gifts? He can minister and sing.*

Then I realized, I've got two good gifts, too. I can minister, plus I'm good at picking Spanish-speaking ministers with many talents!

You see, there is always a way for us to feel good about ourselves without comparing or competing. You can feel good about yourself right where you are. You have an anointing to be you. The good news is, nobody can be a better you than you.

## Consider This

When we give Jesus our absolute best, of our time, our talent, and our resources, it is an act of worship. We are saying with our actions, "God, You mean more to me than anything. Because You are so awesome, I want to give You everything that I am." It pleases Jesus when we come to Him with an open and humble heart. When we draw near to Him, He draws near to us. When you give Him your best, He gives You His best in return.

---
---
---
---
---
---
---

Men are never duly touched and impressed with a conviction of their insignificance until they have contrasted themselves with the majesty of God.

—John Calvin

---
---
---
---

_____

_____
_____

_____

## What the Scriptures Say

If the whole body were an eye, where would the sense of hearing be? If the whole body were an ear, where would the sense of smell be? But in fact God has placed the parts in the body, every one of them, just as he wanted them to be.

—1 Corinthians 12:17–18 (NIV)

This was John's testimony when the Jewish leaders sent priests and Temple assistants from Jerusalem to ask John, "Who are you?" He came right out and said, "I am not the Messiah."

"Well then, who are you?" they asked. "Are you Elijah?"

"No," he replied.

"Are you the Prophet we are expecting?"

"No."

"Then who are you? We need an answer for those who sent us. What do you have to say about yourself?"

John replied in the words of the prophet Isaiah:

"I am a voice shouting in the wilderness,

'Clear the way for the LORD's coming!'"

—John 1:19–23 (NLT)

## A Prayer for Today

Heavenly Father, thank You for loving me. Thank You for choosing me. I ask that You help me to know my limitations. Help me to know my place in the body of Christ so that I can bring glory and honor to You. In Jesus' name. Amen.

_____

_____

_____

_____

_____

_____

_____

Do not be awe struck by other people and try to copy them.
Nobody can be you as efficiently as you can.

—Norman Vincent Peale

_____

_____

_____

_____

_____

_____

_____

### Takeaway Truth

There will always be someone ahead of us that
is more of this or that. Learn to be the best that
you can be and celebrate who God has made you
to be. Learn not to be jealous of others; instead,
celebrate what is going on in their lives. If you
desire to fulfill your God-given destiny and
reach your full potential, learn to stay focused
on who God has called you to be and you will
find happiness in each day.

# DAY 5

## Celebrate Yourself and the Success of Others

. . . . . . . . . . . . . . . . . . . . . . . . . . . . . . . . . . . . . . . . . . . . . . . .

*Key Truth*

When you are happy with yourself, you can
be happy for others.

. . . . . . . . . . . . . . . . . . . . . . . . . . . . . . . . . . . . . . . . . . . . . . . .

The first time Victoria and I went to Billy Graham's home to visit him and Ruth, we were so honored. When we walked into the living room and saw Billy Graham sitting in a chair, it was like seeing Moses. He is one of the heroes of our faith. I've always had the utmost respect and admiration for him. I have looked up to him and held him in awe. It was an honor to meet this giant of our faith.

As I shook his hand, he said, "I love watching you on television, and I just so admire how you can take that message of hope around the world."

*That is so amazing*, I thought. *I've admired him my whole life, and somehow he's found something in me to appreciate.*

Billy has a very gracious personality, but we all need to believe that we are special. You are anointed in your own unique way. You are gifted. You have accomplishments. You may tend to see how great everybody else is, but let me tell you, there is something great about you. Somebody thinks you're amazing. Someone else is inspired by your life. Some even wish they could be you. You are a person to be celebrated. So put your shoulders back. Hold your head up high. You don't have to compete with anyone else. Just be the best you can be.

This is one of the things that threw King Saul off-track. He was doing fine. Samuel had anointed him to be king. His future looked very bright. But he didn't understand this principle.

One day he and David were in a battle. They defeated the Philistines. Everything was great until some of the women said, "Saul has slain his thousands, and David his tens of thousands" (1 Samuel 18:7 niv).

First Samuel 18:9–10 says Saul was very angry and jealous; he never again looked at David the same way. Saul was so insecure that David's success made him feel inferior. You'd think King Saul would be thrilled to have someone as skilled as David on his team. But it takes a secure person to say, "Even though I'm ahead of you, I will let you shine. I'll let you rise higher."

The real test as to whether God continues to promote you is how well you handle the successes of others. Can you celebrate what God is doing in their lives and not be jealous and critical, or feel you are in competition with them?

Saul lost the kingdom, in part, because he could not tolerate anyone being celebrated more than him. A spirit of competition, pride, or jealousy will cause us to do things we never dreamed we would do.

Prior to that jealousy, Saul loved David. He treated him like a son. He took him into the palace. David ate dinner with Saul and his family every night. Saul never dreamed that one day he would throw a javelin at David and try to kill him. He never imagined that one day he would hunt him down in the wilderness.

What was his problem? Saul couldn't handle being number two. He couldn't stand the fact that David's reputation as a warrior had grown greater than his. Saul should have been like John the Baptist and said, "Hey, this is what I am, and this is what I'm not, and I'm okay with that."

If Saul had just been satisfied with his gift and run his race, he could have fulfilled his God-given destiny. But instead, he grew distracted.

He wasted his time and energy competing with someone who was not even in his race. God had already ordained David to go further.

## Consider This

Remember, you don't have to impress anybody. You don't have to prove who you are. You are a child of the Most High God, anointed, equipped, empowered. Keep your shoulders back. Keep your head held high. Be secure in who God made you to be. If you will stay free from a spirit of competition and just run your race you'll not only enjoy your life more, but you'll also see your gifts and talents come out to the full. Because when you celebrate others, God will celebrate you.

_____

_____

_____

_____

_____

_____

_____

Self-confidence is the first requisite to great undertakings.
—Samuel Johnson

_____

_____

_____

_____

_____

_____

_____

## What the Scriptures Say

"Please take this gift I have brought you, for God has been very gracious to me. I have more than enough." And because Jacob insisted, Esau finally accepted the gift.

—Genesis 33:11 (NLT)

Freely you have received; freely give.

—Matthew 10:8 (NIV)

## A Prayer for Today

Father God, thank You for giving me so much. Thank You for blessing me with talents and abilities and the desire to bless others. Show me ways to reach out and help others move forward and help them be successful so we can all rise higher together.

_____

_____

_____

_____

_____

_____

_____

_____

Without a humble but reasonable confidence in your own powers you cannot be successful or happy.

—Norman Vincent Peale

_____

_____

_____

_____

_____

_____

_____

_____

_____

### *Takeaway Truth*

One of life's tests requires learning to celebrate
the success of others. You may be tempted to be
jealous or critical when someone rises higher,
passing you up, whether it's in the office,
on a team, or in an organization.

# DAY 6

## Surround Yourself with Believers

*Key Truth*

To be all that God created you to be, you need
people who support and encourage you.

Scripture shares the story (see Mark 5:22–24, 35–43) of a man named Jairus who pleaded with Jesus to come to his house where his daughter lay dying and heal her. Jesus and the man were on their way when word came by messenger: "You don't need to come. She has already died."

But Jesus replied, "Don't worry about it. She'll be okay. We're coming anyway."

Jesus would not let anyone go with Him except Peter, James, and John. They were members of His inner circle. Now the others with Him were good people, too. They loved the Lord. But Jesus said, "I only want these three to go."

Why was that? Jesus knew when He entered the room where the little girl was dead, He needed to be surrounded by true believers who would not question who He was or what He intended to do. Jesus did not need doubters or skeptics asking, "Are You sure You're the Son of God? Have You ever done this before? What if it doesn't work? Do You have a backup plan?"

When you are in the heat of the battle and need God's favor, you can't afford to have naysayers and doubters in your inner circle. Jesus did not need to hear things like, "Do You really think she'll get well? My grandmother died of that same thing."

We all need people who are joined in spirit with us and say, "If you're bold enough to believe, count me in. I'm bold enough to agree with you."

You need supporters who will come into agreement with you and release their faith, not doubters who tell you what you can't do.

When Jesus entered the child's room, all those gathered were distraught and weeping.

"Don't be upset. She's not dead," Jesus said. "She's only asleep."

Some mourners turned on Jesus, mocking Him.

His response is one of the keys to living a life of victory. Mark 5:40 says, "They laughed and jeered at Him. But [Jesus] put them all out" (AMP).

Jesus showed them the door. His attitude was, "I don't need your doubt."

If you find yourself surrounded by people who mock and doubt you, show them the door just as Jesus did.

He didn't allow anyone into the room except the girl's parents and His inner circle. He then spoke to the child and she came back to life. Jesus could have healed her in front of the laughing and mocking crowd. He's the Son of God. He could do anything.

But I believe Jesus wanted to make the point that your inner circle is extremely important. If Jesus took the time to weed out the doubters, surely you and I should be that concerned about our own inner circles.

Are those in your inner circle building you up or tearing you down? Are they inspiring you to go further, or are they telling you what you can't do? Are they modeling excellence, integrity, generosity, and godliness? Or are they lazy compromisers, going nowhere? Don't waste your time with anyone who drags you down instead of making you better.

## Consider This

I can't think of anything worse than to come to the end of life and realize that someone you trusted kept you from becoming the person God created you to be. You may be fearful of losing a friend and being lonely, but you never give up something for God that He doesn't make up for by giving you something better in return. If you'll make the change, God will not only give you new friends, He will give you better friends—friends who will celebrate you and help you become who God has created you to be.

_____

_____

_____

_____

_____

_____

_____

_____

One doesn't know, till one is a bit at odds with the world, how much one's friends who believe in one rather generously, mean to one.

—D. H. Lawrence

_____

_____

_____

_____

_____

_____

_____

## What the Scriptures Say

While Jesus was still speaking, some people came from the house of Jairus, the synagogue leader. "Your daughter is dead," they said. "Why bother the teacher anymore?"

Overhearing what they said, Jesus told him, "Don't be afraid; just believe."

He did not let anyone follow him except Peter, James and John the brother of James. When they came to the home of the synagogue leader, Jesus saw a commotion, with people crying and wailing loudly. He went in and said to them, "Why all this commotion and wailing? The child is not dead but asleep." But they laughed at him.

After he put them all out, he took the child's father and mother and the disciples who were with him, and went in where the child was. He took her by the hand and said to her, "*Talitha koum!*" (which means "Little girl, I say to you, get up!"). Immediately the girl stood up and began to walk around (she was twelve years old). At this they were completely astonished. He gave strict orders not to let anyone know about this, and told them to give her something to eat.

—Mark 5:35–43 (NIV)

Do not give dogs what is sacred; do not throw your pearls to pigs. If you do, they may trample them under their feet, and turn and tear you to pieces.

—Matthew 7:6 (NIV)

## A Prayer for Today

Father, I humbly come to You today asking that You remove anyone from my inner circle who would keep me from being what You intend me to be. Please put in place those who will help me fulfill

Your plan for my life so that I can move forward into all You have in store for me.

_____

_____

_____

_____

_____

_____

_____

_____

She is a friend of mind. She gather me, man. The pieces I am,
she gather them and give them back to me in all the right order.

—Toni Morrison

_____

_____

_____

_____

_____

_____

_____

_____

### Takeaway Truth

The people in your inner circle should believe in
you. They should celebrate your gifts and push
you ahead, not hold you back.

# Iron Sharpens Iron

*Key Truth*

You cannot soar with the eagles as long as you're hanging out with the turkeys. So rid yourself of relationships that drain you, drag you down, or leave you feeling worse for the wear.

I expect that people in need will come to me in my role as a minister. I welcome them and try to help in any way I can. That said, there are some people who just keep coming back for more. These negative, needy people constantly dump their problems on your doorstep and expect you to clean them up. They know only one song, and it's sad. After crying with them through eight or nine verses, you realize they don't want to be helped or encouraged. They just want to unload on you. They bask in the attention. They suck the energy right out of you. Spend an hour with them, and you'll feel like you've run a marathon.

Needy people can abuse your kindness. Sometimes, you have to put up with their difficulties and love them back to wholeness, but you can't spend your whole life knee-deep in their troubles. You have a God-given destiny to fulfill. I've found that in some cases the best help you can give negative, needy people is to not help them at all. Otherwise, you are just enabling their dysfunction.

When I was in my early twenties, just a couple of months ago

(Don't laugh!), I regularly went to a very nice, good-hearted young lady for my haircuts. Unfortunately, every snip of the scissors brought another tale of woe. She unloaded on me even as she trimmed me up. Month after month, year after year, she poured into my ears her stories of being mistreated by her bosses, her relatives, and her girl-friends, and on and on.

Every time I left her shop I had less hair, but my head felt heavier. I was depressed. She was a very good sad storyteller. She reminded me of the guy who was about to jump off a bridge and end his life. A good Samaritan ran over to save him, saying, "Don't jump! Don't jump! Tell your troubles to me instead!"

Two hours later, they both jumped.

That's the way this young lady was. I did my best to encourage her. I would pray with her. I gave her money. I sent her custom-ers. It was never enough. One day I realized what I'm telling you: I could not go where God was taking me with her in my life. I love her. I pray for her. I miss her good haircuts, but I couldn't fulfill my God-given destiny with her putting poison in my ears month after month.

So, I made a change.

## Consider This

Proverbs 27:17 says, "As iron sharpens iron, so a friend sharpens a friend" (NLT). Are your friends making you stronger? Are they chal-lenging you to become a better parent, a better spouse, a better co-worker, a better member of your community?

If not, you may have to change where you do business, where you play ball, where you work, where you shop. Your time on this earth is brief and valuable. You have a destiny to fulfill, and you can't make it happen if you are carrying needy and negative people on your back. The solution is found in Mark 5:40, which explains how Jesus "put out" those who doubted Him. Show them the door. Be kind. Be polite. But pull away.

_____

_____

_____

_____

_____

_____

_____

_____

The antidote for fifty enemies is one friend.

—Aristotle

_____

_____

_____

_____

_____

_____

_____

## What the Scriptures Say

Above all, love each other deeply, because love covers over a multitude of sins.

—I Peter 4:8 (NIV)

Perfume and incense bring joy to the heart, and the pleasantness of a friend springs from their heartfelt advice.

—Proverbs 27:9 (NIV)

_____

_____

_____

_____

_____

_____

_____

_____

_____

## A Prayer for Today

Father God, thank You for the people You have placed in my life. Help me to see them the way You see them. Help me to appreciate the ways we sharpen one another so that we can help each other fulfill Your plan for our lives.

> In everyone's life, at some time, our inner fire goes out. It is then burst into flame by an encounter with another human being. We should all be thankful for those people who rekindle the inner spirit.
>
> —Albert Schweitzer

_____

_____

_____

_____

_____

_____

_____

_____

_____

## *Takeaway Truth*

If you are to be happy and enjoy your relationships, you need to learn how to appreciate the differences and learn from the people in your life. If you don't focus on the right things, you'll end up allowing the little irritations to cause you to become resentful. Remember, nobody is perfect. If you're to grow, you must be willing to overlook some things. Our assignment is not to fix people. Our assignment is to love people. Our assignment is to sharpen one another so we can move forward in the good plan God has prepared for us.

# STEP FOUR

*Travel Light*

# DAY 1

## Let Your Bruises Heal

*Key Truth*

When you forgive others, you take away
their power to hurt you.

We all have unfair things happen to us. We can choose to cling to that hurt and let it destroy our day-to-day happiness and poison our futures, or we can choose to release the hurt and trust God to make it up to us. You may think you can't forgive those who've hurt you, whether they are friends, a spouse, or co-workers. But you don't have to forgive them for their sakes; you forgive for your own sake.

The mistake we make so often is to hold on to hurt. We go around bitter and angry, but all we're doing is allowing those who hurt us to control our lives. The abuser, bully, or critic isn't hurt by our anger and bitterness. We're just poisoning our own lives with it.

I know people who are still mad at others who are long dead and gone. They're still bitter at their parents or a former boss or an ex-spouse who is no longer living. It's bad enough that someone hurt you once; don't let them continue to hurt you by staying angry. When you forgive someone, you set a prisoner free. That prisoner isn't the person who hurt you; the prisoner is you.

Someone may have lied about you, betrayed you, or mistreated you, but what they did was not enough to keep you from your destiny. You cannot let one divorce, one betrayal, or one bad childhood experience keep you from the awesome future God has in store for you.

In the Bible, Joseph's brothers betrayed him. They sold him into slavery. He could have been angry and let that one bad break, that one injustice, steal his destiny, but he let it go and moved forward to claim his rewards. There is no telling how many people in Joseph's time were kept from God's best because they went for revenge instead.

Don't let that be you. Your destiny is too great to let what someone did to you keep you from moving forward. Forgiveness is not about being nice and kind, it's about letting go so you can claim the amazing future that awaits you.

I know there are valid reasons to be angry. Maybe you were mistreated at a young age. It wasn't your fault. You had no control over it, and what was done to you was wrong. Forgiving doesn't mean you're excusing anything or anyone. It doesn't mean you're lessening the offense. I'm not saying you have to go be friends with someone who hurt you. I'm simply saying to let it go for your own sake. Quit dwelling on the offense. Quit replaying it in your memory. Quit giving it time and energy.

When you hold on to a hurt, you never let it heal. It's like a bruise that won't go away. If you've ever hit your arm and bruised it and then had someone bump it, you know how it hurts. You pull back because the bruised area is very sensitive. You become overly protective and you make sure no one gets close. In the same way, when you've been bruised emotionally, you tend to be overly sensitive. If your hurt isn't allowed to heal, the smallest bump will cause you to be defensive. You can't develop healthy relationships while your emotional bruises remain unhealed.

There's nothing the enemy would love any more than for you to let one bad thing that happened—one messed-up person who did you wrong, or one injustice—ruin the rest of your life. Put your foot down and say, "My destiny is too great, my future is too bright, and my God is too big to let an old hurt cause me to be sour and bitter and stuck where I am. No, I'll shake it off and press forward into the bright future God has in store for me."

## Consider This

The Scripture says that Jesus was sent "to announce release to the captives...to send forth as delivered those who are oppressed [who are downtrodden, bruised, crushed, and broken down by calamity]" (Luke 4:18 AMP). This indicates that when we're bruised, we're not free. Unfair things happen to all of us. If you want to see that bruise go away and walk into the freedom God has in store for you, you have to forgive the wrongs. You have to let go of what somebody did and move forward with your life.

_____

_____

_____

_____

_____

_____

_____

_____

Always forgive your enemies—nothing annoys them so much.

—Oscar Wilde

_____

_____

_____

_____

_____

_____

_____

_____

## What the Scriptures Say

The Spirit of the Lord is upon me, because he hath anointed me to preach the gospel to the poor; he hath sent me to heal the brokenhearted, to preach deliverance to the captives, and recovering of sight to the blind, to set at liberty them that are bruised, to preach the acceptable year of the Lord.

—Luke 4:18–19 (KJV)

Get rid of all bitterness, rage and anger, brawling and slander, along with every form of malice. Be kind and compassionate to one another, forgiving each other, just as in Christ God forgave you.

—Ephesians 4:31–32 (NIV)

## A Prayer for Today

Heavenly Father, thank You for forgiving me and setting me free. Today I choose to forgive others so that I can have room in my heart to receive Your forgiveness and love.

_____

_____

_____

_____

_____

_____

_____

There is within every soul a thirst for happiness and meaning.

—Thomas Aquinas

_____

_____

_____

_____

_____

_____

_____

_____

_____

### Takeaway Truth

You have a destiny to fulfill. You have a
joyful life to claim. Every time you let past
hurts consume your thoughts, you are just
reopening an old wound.

# DAY 2

## *A God of Justice*

### *Key Truth*

When you can pray for your enemies
and even bless those who do you wrong,
God will settle your accounts.

································································

Les was raised in a very abusive environment. His father was an alcoholic and he would come home in these violent rages. Les was afraid his dad would hurt his mom or him. He was afraid for his life.

There was no peace in his home. He lived constantly on edge. One night his dad came home drunk and started abusing his mother, not only verbally but also physically. Les was fourteen years old. He stepped up and told his dad to leave his mom alone. They fought and in the end his dad threw him out of the house.

"I don't want to ever see your face again," his father told him. "If you ever set foot in this house again, it will be the last time you ever do it."

Les was devastated, so despondent he considered ending his life. He was standing on a bridge in the middle of the night about to jump when something unexpected stopped him. Les had never been to church. Religion was not part of his life. But suddenly he heard a voice say, "Don't do it. I'll be your Father. I'll be your Protector. I'll take care of you."

At that moment he felt as though warm oil was pouring all over him. It was like something he had never felt before. That was his heavenly Father showing up to bring about justice. The psalmist said, "Although my father and my mother have forsaken me, yet the Lord will take me up [adopt me as His child]" (Psalm 27:10 AMP).

Les was on his own from that day forward. He was filled with all these hurts and pain, so much rejection. But he made a decision at the very beginning that he wasn't going to hate his father. He forgave him and went on with his life.

He became a minister. Les had reached out to his father through the years, but the father wouldn't have anything to do with him. Then, one Sunday morning twenty-two years later, Les was standing in the pulpit and out of the blue in walked his father. It was the first time Les had seen his dad since that night when he was fourteen years old.

At the end of the service his dad walked down to the altar with tears running down his face. He asked his son for forgiveness and also gave his life to the Lord.

God is a God of justice. I don't know how long it will take, but God has promised He'll make the wrongs right. He'll restore what the enemy has stolen. It doesn't matter how badly someone has hurt you. It doesn't matter how wrong they were. If you'll let it go, God will settle your accounts. God will pay you back.

At the end of that service, this dad and son sat down and talked. The father told his son things Les had never known before. The father said his own father was an alcoholic. He'd fought with his own mother growing up. The father's childhood home was so unstable that by the time his dad was six years old, he had already lived with four families.

There was no excuse for his father's behavior, but what I want you to see is that hurting people hurt others. Les's father had all that anger and abuse on the inside, and he made the mistake of carrying it around. He didn't realize he was passing it on to the next generation.

## Consider This

When Jesus rose from the dead and came back to talk with His disciples, He said, "If you forgive the sins of any, they are forgiven them; if you retain the sins of any, they are retained" (John 20:23 NKJV). When you retain a sin, you hold on to it. God was saying that when you hold on to the wrongs people have done to you, then the poison contaminates *you*. When you don't forgive, it's easy to become what you hate.

_____

_____

_____

_____

_____

_____

_____

_____

_____

Forgiveness is the fragrance the violet sheds on the heel that has crushed it.

—Mark Twain

_____

_____

_____

_____

_____

_____

_____

_____

## What the Scriptures Say

If you forgive the sins of any, their sins have been forgiven them; if you retain the sins of any, they have been retained.

—John 20:23 (NASB)

Even if my father and mother abandon me, the LORD will hold me close.

—Psalm 27:10 (NLT)

## A Prayer for Today

Father, I know the person was wrong to hurt me. It was not fair, but God, I'm not looking for revenge. I ask You, God, to heal them and give them what they need.

_____

_____

_____

_____

_____

_____

_____

To forgive is to set a prisoner free and discover that the prisoner was you.

—Lewis B. Smedes

_____

_____

_____

_____

_____

_____

_____

### Takeaway Truth

It will help you to forgive if you'll realize that the
people who hurt you have problems and issues.
Hurting people hurt others. When somebody
lashes out at you or treats you unfairly, it's a
sign they have unresolved issues of their own.
There's no excuse for hurting you, but they are
part of a chain that needs to be broken.
Somebody hurt them, so they hurt you.
Take a merciful approach and forgive them.

# A New Season Will Come

*Key Truth*
Our God is a God
of new beginnings.

I was in my backyard talking to Manny, who helps with our landscaping. This was the middle of winter and the grass was very brown. It looked dead. I told Manny that I feared the lawn was dead and he said, "It doesn't look very good, but the truth is the grass is not really dead. It's just not in season. In the spring, this same grass will be lush and green."

That's the way it is in life. Sometimes our dreams appear to be dead or dying. But you have to realize, they are not really dead. They are just not in season. They are coming back. New seasons of growth are coming. New health. New relationships. New opportunities. Just because something looks dead, don't write it off.

When you go through disappointments and setbacks, instead of being down and discouraged and giving up, have the attitude of *It may not look good, but I know the truth. It's not really dead. It's just not in season. I'm in wintertime, but I know springtime is coming. So I will lift up my head and get ready for the new things God is about to do.*

If you want to overcome discouragement, learn how to transition into the different seasons of life. The Scripture tells us of a lady named Naomi who didn't do this very well. She failed to realize that just because a season was over, it didn't mean her life was over.

Often we want a certain season to last forever, but that may not be how God has it planned. You have to be open and willing to adapt and adjust when changes come. Do not be bitter when something happens that you don't like or don't understand.

Of course, no one likes to go through traumatic changes or loss or disappointment, but it's all a part of life. In those difficult seasons, you have to remind yourself that God is still on the throne, and the fact that the grass looks dead doesn't mean it will never be green again.

Naomi was going along just great. Life was good. But over time she went through a series of losses. Her husband died. Later, her two sons died. It's difficult to go through a loss. There is a proper time for grieving. But you have to make sure you don't let a season of mourning turn into a lifetime of mourning.

Naomi made the mistake of letting the bitterness and the discouragement remain inside her. She despaired and lost all happiness. She didn't think the grass would ever be green again. She actually changed her name to Mara, which means "sorrow," because she wanted to be reminded of her pain and misery every time someone called her name.

Naomi's attitude was, *All my dreams have been shattered. I'm never going to be happy again. Just leave me in my trouble and heartache.*

Obviously, I do not recommend you follow the path taken by Naomi. When you suffer a loss, a disappointment, an unfair situation, you have to make sure that you don't let your circumstances rob you of happiness for the rest of your life.

After suffering so much, Naomi moved back to her hometown with her daughter-in-law Ruth. There, Ruth met a man, fell in love, and was married. Eventually, Ruth had a son. By then Naomi was an old woman. But when she saw that little baby boy, something lit up on the inside.

She felt a new sense of purpose, a new sense of destiny. As she was holding the baby, something amazing happened. Milk began to be produced in her body. The Scripture says this older woman, way up in her senior years, was able to nurse the little baby. Naomi was just as happy and fulfilled as she could be. She discovered that spring always comes after winter. Bad times do not last forever.

## Consider This

God has set up seasons in our lives. If you're not making as much progress as you would like, the key is to not lose any ground. Keep a good attitude and do the right thing, even when it's hard. When you do that, you are passing the test, and God promises that your due season is coming. Be encouraged because your appointed time of increase, favor, and promotion is on its way, and He will fulfill every dream and desire He's placed within your heart!

_____

_____

_____

_____

_____

_____

_____

_____

No matter how long the winter, spring is sure to follow.

—Proverb

_____

_____

_____

_____

_____

_____

_____

_____

## What the Scriptures Say

For everything there is a season, a time for every activity under heaven.

—Ecclesiastes 3:1 (NLT)

I will give you rain in due season, and the land shall yield her increase and the trees of the field yield their fruit.

—Leviticus 26:4 (AMP)

## A Prayer for Today

Father God, I bless You today. I thank You for preparing me for the season of promotion You have in my future. I surrender my heart, mind, will, and emotions to You so that I can live as a testimony of Your work in my life.

_____

_____

_____

_____

_____

_____

_____

Where man sees but withered leaves, God sees sweet flowers growing.

—Albert Laighton

_____

_____

_____

_____

_____

_____

_____

_____

_____

· · · · · · · · · · · · · · · · · · · · · · · · · · · · · · · · · · · · · ·

### *Takeaway Truth*

Remember, God is good. If you refuse to live in
discouragement, if you lift your head and rise
from your despair, you will discover, as Naomi
did, that the ending of one season in your life
does not mean the ending of your entire life.

· · · · · · · · · · · · · · · · · · · · · · · · · · · · · · · · · · · · · ·

# DAY 4

## Do Not Panic in Times of Turmoil

. . . . . . . . . . . . . . . . . . . . . . . . . . . . . . . . . . . . . . . . . . . . . . . . . . . .

*Key Truth*
Turbulent times do not last,
so hang on to your faith.

. . . . . . . . . . . . . . . . . . . . . . . . . . . . . . . . . . . . . . . . . . . . . . . . . . . .

I was on a flight to India with my father years ago when the friendly skies turned mean. We had been flying for about thirteen hours. We had another couple of hours to go. Up to that point the flight had been very smooth and comfortable. But at one point we hit some turbulence like nothing I had ever experienced.

This was worse than the worst roller coaster. The plane was going every which way. Food and bags went flying, hitting the ceiling, passengers, and the floor. For ten minutes it was the wildest ride of my life. People were hollering. Babies were crying. That plane was shaking so violently, we were sure the whole thing was breaking apart.

Being the great man of faith that I am, I thought, *This is it. It's over. There is no way we will survive.*

Yes, I surrendered my happiness and joy to sheer, unadulterated panic.

The turbulence seemed to last an eternity, but sure enough, in about ten minutes we were through it and returned to a calm and smooth ride. Two hours later we landed safely at our destination.

That's the way it is in life. One minute you are happy and filled with contentment, doing just fine. You have a good job, healthy children, and you are feeling blessed. Then you hit some turbulence. Your routine medical tests turn up a problem. Your relationship becomes rocky. A lawsuit is filed.

The challenge is to keep looking ahead, knowing that the turbulence will not last forever, that one day soon, happiness will be possible. At the time, you may feel the good life is over, but take it from me, this, too, shall pass.

My theory is that every person has at least ten minutes of brain-rattling turbulence in life. Usually, the scary moments don't come all at once. You may experience a minute here, five minutes there, a couple of minutes down the road. In those tough times when you feel like the plane is breaking apart and panic overwhelms you, go to your faith. Trust that the Creator of the universe is piloting your plane. The Most High God is directing your steps. Remember that He said no weapon formed against you will prosper. God said not to be surprised by these fiery trials. Do not panic. Go to that place of peace even in the midst of turbulence.

## Consider This

God is still on the throne. He has brought you this far. Your life may have taken a plunge and you may feel like you've been put through a giant mixer. Others around you may be panicked. But sooner or later, calm will be restored.

_____

_____

_____

_____

_____

_____

_____

_____

Pain is inevitable. Suffering is optional.

—M. Kathleen Casey

---

---

---

---

---

---

---

## What the Scriptures Say

He who was seated on the throne said, "I am making everything new!"

—Revelation 21:5 (NIV)

This is what the LORD says: "Restrain your voice from weeping and your eyes from tears, for your work will be rewarded," declares the LORD. "They will return from the land of the enemy."

—Jeremiah 31:16 (NIV)

## A Prayer for Today

Father, in the most turbulent times I will keep believing for good things and blessings in the future because I know this, too, will pass.

---

---

---

---

---

_____

_____

If you're going through hell, keep going.

—Winston Churchill

_____

_____

_____

_____

_____

_____

_____

_____

_____

### Takeaway Truth

I've heard it said, "Trouble is inevitable, but
misery is optional." Trouble descends on all of
us from time to time, but we can decide whether
to fall apart or pull it together. We have that
power, even when we are blindsided.

## DAY 5

# Your Weeds Will Become Wheat

*Key Truth*

Unexpected challenges will arise just when you are about to be victorious; but if you stay in faith and persevere, victory will come.

In Matthew 13:24–30, Jesus tells a story about a man who planted wheat. He sowed good seed, doing the right thing, honoring God, being good to others. But while he slept an enemy came and planted weeds in his soil. He was expecting to have a great harvest of wheat. He had sown good seed, but when it came time for harvest, weeds sprang up among his wheat.

Don't be surprised if things turn bad on you even as you do the right things, honor God, and work to be your best every day. It may not seem fair, but the enemy is spreading weeds among your wheat, just as was done to this farmer.

The workers said to the farmer, "Where did these weeds come from? We saw you. We know you sowed good seeds."

The farmer said, "An enemy has come in and sown these destructive seeds."

The good news is, those weeds do not have to keep you from your God-given destiny. Scripture says when the wheat was ready for harvest, the weeds sprang up unexpectedly. The message is that when you are close to victory, when you are on the verge of your greatest accomplishment and your greatest breakthrough, that's when the unexpected challenges will pop up as the enemy tries to keep you from moving forward.

Jack and Megan were delighted when their first son Ronnie was born, but by the time he was two years old, they knew the boy was not developing normally. He was eventually diagnosed with severe autism. Their doctor suggested Jack and Megan go to a counselor to help them deal with this unexpected challenge, but they didn't dwell on any sadness. They were too busy arranging to get Ronnie enrolled in the best programs.

Their next child, Charlie, was born two years later. To their initial relief, he appeared to be a normal child. In his first few years, Jack and Megan thought they'd been blessed with an exceptionally bright son for all the love they'd given Ronnie. But then Charlie, too, began to show symptoms of autism. His development stalled.

Again, Jack and Megan refused to give up their happiness to despair. They poured all of their energy into helping their boys be the best they could be, so they could lead the best possible lives. The couple grew closer than they'd ever been as they joined forces to serve the needs of their sons.

When asked how they managed to stay positive and to hang on to their happiness despite the challenges they faced as parents, Jack and Megan said, "We just never felt we were alone in this. We knew He would not give us more than we could handle. We always believed God would be there for us, and that this was part of His plan for our family."

I encourage you to see unexpected challenges in a new light. Instead of falling apart and giving up your happiness to despair, know that God will take care of it for you.

The parable of the weeds and the wheat ends with the workers asking the farmer, "Should we go out and pull up the weeds?"

"No. Just wait and at the right time the weeds will be destroyed," the farmer said.

## Consider This

God is saying to you that you don't have to spend your life constantly trying to pull the weeds that pop up. If you do that, you will destroy the harvest, too.

_____

_____

_____

_____

_____

_____

_____

We acquire the strength we have overcome.

—Ralph Waldo Emerson

_____

_____

_____

_____

_____

_____

_____

## What the Scriptures Say

Jesus told them another parable: "The kingdom of heaven is like a man who sowed good seed in his field. But while everyone was sleeping, his enemy came and sowed weeds among the wheat, and went away. When the wheat sprouted and formed heads, then the weeds also appeared.

"The owner's servants came to him and said, 'Sir, didn't you sow good seed in your field? Where then did the weeds come from?'

"'An enemy did this,' he replied.

"The servants asked him, 'Do you want us to go and pull them up?'

"'No,' he answered, 'because while you are pulling the weeds, you may uproot the wheat with them. Let both grow together until the harvest. At that time I will tell the harvesters: First collect the weeds and tie them in bundles to be burned; then gather the wheat and bring it into my barn.'"

—Matthew 13:24–30 (NIV)

Dear friends, don't be surprised at the fiery trials you are going through, as if something strange were happening to you.

—1 Peter 4:12 (NLT)

## A Prayer for Today

Father God, I ask that You help me stay in faith during difficult times so that I can reap the abundant harvest You have in store for me.

_____

_____

_____

_____

_____

_____

_____

I know God will not give me anything I can't handle. I just wish that He didn't trust me so much.

—Mother Teresa

_____

_____

_____

_____

_____

_____

_____

### *Takeaway Truth*

We have to wake up every day and set our minds
on God's Word and choose to speak His truth
over our lives. We have to remain in faith during
difficult stretches so that we can reap a good
harvest in the future.

# DAY 6

## *See the Good*

*Key Truth*

A critical spirit taints everything, so train yourself to see the good.

I grew up with a woman who has been critical as long as I've known her. Even as a teenager she complained about things at school that I didn't even think about. I never knew I had it so bad until she told me. I heard just the other day (and this is thirty years since high school), that she just left another job, upset, saying the people didn't treat her right. The sad thing is, she will go through the rest of her life bitter and frustrated if she doesn't change her way of viewing life.

Parents, it's important that we break any critical, faultfinding spirit we find in ourselves so we don't pass it down to our children. That's what happened with this young lady. I remember going over to her house when we were kids. Her parents were the same way. They were always critical about something; critical of the city, critical of their neighbors. The father was critical of his employer. The mother was always complaining about the place where she worked.

The solution to overcoming a critical spirit is, number one, to recognize when your way of viewing life is tainted. Number two, just as you've developed a habit of seeing the worst, retrain yourself to see the good.

A few months ago I met a young man with his girlfriend after a service. They had more piercings and tattoos than any two people I've ever seen. The man had tattoos up and down his arms, all over his neck, and even on his face. The young lady must have had a hundred piercings.

They definitely did not look like our usual visitors. When you see people whose appearance is out of the ordinary, that critical spirit tries to rise up and make you think, *Why do they look like that? They must have some real issues.*

But instead of seeing them through my critical eyes, I looked at them through God's eyes. When I did that I had a different perspective. I was glad they felt comfortable coming to our church. I was glad they took time to honor God.

When I talked to them, I realized they weren't anything like I'd expected. They were the kindest, most respectful people you could ever meet. On the outside you could find a thousand reasons to be judgmental or critical. A *religious* attitude wants to point out all the faults and ask: *Who do they think they are, and what's their problem?*

But what better place for them to be than in church? Come to find out, this young man was the leader of a very successful heavy-metal band. They'd had a big concert at the arena the night before. He looked to be about thirty years old. He said, "I've never been to church in my life. This is my first time to ever set foot in a place of worship."

He gave me one of his CDs and told me to listen to track seven.

"That's a song I wrote from listening to you," he said.

Don't judge people by their outside appearance. When you're tempted to be critical and find fault, remember that the enemy is called "the accuser of our brethren" (Revelation 12:10 NKJV). Recognize the source of your criticism. That's who's giving you the desire. I don't know about you, but I'm not getting on the side of the accuser; I'm staying on God's side. I'm believing the best.

There may be a thousand things wrong, but I'm going to search until I find the one thing that's right. I've been forgiven much, so I try to love even more. If I err, I'm not erring on the side of judgment; I'm erring on the side of mercy.

## Consider This

A critical spirit follows you everywhere you go. You can't get away from it. But if you don't deal with whatever is tainting your view of the world, you'll have the same problems over and over again.

_____

_____

_____

_____

_____

_____

_____

The sun shines and warms and lights us and we have no curiosity to know why this is so; but we ask the reason of all evil, of pain, and hunger, and mosquitoes and silly people.

—Ralph Waldo Emerson

_____

_____

_____

_____

_____

_____

_____

## What the Scriptures Say

We have not stopped praying for you since we first heard about you. We ask God to give you complete knowledge of his will and to give you spiritual wisdom and understanding. Then the way you live will always honor and please the Lord, and your lives will produce every kind of good fruit. All the while, you will grow as you learn to know God better and better.

We also pray that you will be strengthened with all his glorious power so you will have all the endurance and patience you need. May you be filled with joy.

—Colossians 1:9–11 (NLT)

In your relationships with one another, have the same mindset as Christ Jesus.

—Philippians 2:5 (NIV)

## A Prayer for Today

Father, today I choose to have a positive, faith-filled view of the world. I choose to bless You and trust You, even when things don't make sense in my natural mind. I know You have a good plan for me and trust that You are working all things out for my good.

_____

_____

_____

_____

_____

_____

_____

A person who has good thoughts cannot ever be ugly. You can have a wonky nose and a crooked mouth and a double chin and stick-out teeth, but if you have good thoughts they will shine out of your face like sunbeams and you will always look lovely.

—Roald Dahl

_____

_____

_____

_____

_____

_____

_____

_____

_____

· · · · · · · · · · · · · · · · · · · · · · · · · · · · · · · · · · · · · · · · · · ·

### *Takeaway Truth*

When the temptation comes to be critical,
catch yourself. You have to deal with negative
thoughts one at a time. If you see something
or someone you don't understand or you don't
agree with, don't be quick to judge. Don't allow
that critical spirit to come out.

· · · · · · · · · · · · · · · · · · · · · · · · · · · · · · · · · · · · · · · · · · ·

# DAY 7

## *Believe in the Best*

*Key Truth*
Rather than judging others, it's better
to seek understanding.

When I was in high school a young man moved to our city and joined the basketball team. He was a very good athlete, but he was extremely quiet. He had a different personality. We all thought he was odd. He never laughed with us. He just stayed over in the corner and did his own thing, never really joining in.

One day it was just him and me in the locker room. I had never really spoken to him before. Just to be friendly I said, "Hey! Where did you come from? Where did you grow up?"

I'll never forget how sincere he was. He opened up and told me how he had come from a very dysfunctional home. He had been passed from family to family, six different foster homes in three years. He had all this hurt, pain, and insecurity. Once I understood where he was coming from, I saw him in a whole new light. After that, my friends and I made sure to include him in activities. We went the extra mile to make him feel loved, accepted, welcomed, and part of our team. Over the years, I watched him come out of his shell, become more confident and more secure. By the time we graduated, he was just like the rest of us, as happy and friendly as could be.

When you understand people's stories, it's very easy to understand their outward demeanor. When I found out why my new teammate was the way he was, it changed my perspective. I realized how easy it was for me to be secure and happy. I was raised in a good environment. It was easy for me to be confident and expect good things. I'd been surrounded by loving people all my life. But if I hadn't had that loving family, I don't know how I would have responded.

Too often we judge people based on our own backgrounds and on the experiences we've been through. If we are strong in an area where somebody is weak it's easy to think, *I would never do that. I would never be as unfriendly as that young man. I would never have been divorced. I would never have married that person in the first place.*

You don't know what you would have done in their situation. You haven't walked in their shoes. You weren't raised in their environment. You haven't been through the experiences they've been through.

All of us have strengths, and we all have weaknesses. We are strong in certain areas not because we're great and we just decided to be strong, but because of the grace of God in our lives. I am secure and confident because God blessed me with great parents. I cannot judge the actions of someone who was not blessed in that way.

## Consider This

If not for God's goodness, I could be struggling with an addiction or a bad relationship. I could be insecure, angry, and dealing with all kinds of issues. I'm not judging. I'm showing mercy. I won't be critical. I'll be more understanding. After all, we don't know what people are going through. We should give people room instead of making judgments.

_____

_____

_____

_____
_____
_____
_____
_____
_____
_____

How far you go in life depends on your being tender with the young, compassionate with the aged, sympathetic with the striving and tolerant of the weak and strong. Because someday in your life you will have been all of these.

—George Washington Carver

_____
_____
_____
_____
_____
_____
_____
_____
_____

## What the Scriptures Say

God does not show favoritism but accepts from every nation the one who fears him and does what is right.

—Acts 10:34–35 (NIV)

Be sympathetic, love one another, be compassionate and humble.

—1 Peter 3:8 (NIV)

## A Prayer for Today

Father, today I choose to set my heart and mind on You. I choose to love others the way You have commanded. Give me the strength to walk in Your ways and understand Your love more each day.

_____

_____

_____

_____

_____

_____

You can't live a perfect day without doing something for someone who will never be able to repay you.

—John Wooden

_____

_____

_____

_____

_____

_____

_____

_____

### Takeaway Truth

Instead of being holier than thou and judging
people, our attitude should be: *But for the grace
of God, that could be me.*

# STEP FIVE

*Laugh Often*

# DAY 1

## *Laughter Is Good for You*

*Key Truth*

One of the greatest stress relievers God
has given us is laughter.

When my father was seventy-five years old, he still laughed and kidded just like he did when he was twenty. He was a responsible and serious man, but he knew how to have fun. One time we were in Mexico, walking down the main street of a little town, when an American couple approached my father.

They asked him, "Do you know where the post office is?"

My dad looked at them real strange and said, "No comprende. No comprende. Español, amigo."

They thought, *Oh, no. He only speaks Spanish, too.*

So they said it real dramatically: "*Post Office.*"

Daddy shook his head. "No comprende."

Frustrated, the tourist said it even more dramatically: "*Post office. Mail a letter.*"

Daddy brightened up and said, "Post off*eece*?"

They got real excited, "Yes! Yes! Post off*eece*!"

Then Daddy said, "If you're looking for the post office, it's right around the corner."

That man said, "Boy, I ought to whoop you."

My father believed that the world would be a healthier place if we stressed less and laughed more. He never lost that youthful spirit.

He knew that when people are uptight and on edge, headaches, digestive problems, and lack of energy are just some of the results. They don't sleep well. Much of this would go away if they would just learn how to properly deal with stress. One of the greatest stress relievers God has given us is laughter.

When we're good-natured and full of joy, taking time to laugh and play, it's like taking a good medicine. That's what helps us to stay healthy. People who laugh regularly are 40 percent less likely to have a heart attack than those who don't laugh often. Laughter triggers the right side of the brain, which helps release creativity and helps us to make better decisions.

There is too much sickness in our world today. Much of it is related to sadness. It's directly related to the fact that we don't smile enough. We live uptight and stressed-out lives. But even during trials and hard times, God says to us, "I've got a solution. In difficulties, cheer up. In famine, laugh. Keep your joy." You can laugh your way to victory, to better health and to more energy.

God knows the end of the story. He knows the final outcome. The good news is, you and I win. God always causes us to triumph. We should have a spring in our step, a smile on our face, joy in our hearts, and unshakable faith. God's plan for our lives is for good, and He has the answer to our every question. Knowing this, we can laugh at the days ahead!

## Consider This

When is the last time you had a good, hearty laugh? If it's been awhile, maybe your laugher is rusted and needs to be overhauled! You don't know how much better you would feel and the energy you'd pick up if you'd just lighten up and learn to laugh more often—not once a month, not once a week, but every single day.

_____

_____

_____

_____

_____

_____

_____

The most wasted of all days is one without laughter.

—E. E. Cummings

_____

_____

_____

_____

_____

_____

_____

_____

## What the Scriptures Say

Blessed and fortunate and happy and spiritually prosperous...
are those who hunger and thirst for righteousness (upright-
ness and right standing with God), for they shall be completely
satisfied!

—Matthew 5:6 (AMP)

Sarah said, God has made me to laugh; all who hear will laugh
with me.

—Genesis 21:6 (AMP)

## A Prayer for Today

Father in Heaven, thank You for working in my life. Thank You for Your joy that is my strength.

---
---
---
---
---
---
---

Laughter is an instant vacation.

—Milton Berle

---
---
---
---
---
---
---

### Takeaway Truth

Laughing makes you feel better and releases
healing throughout your system. When
we laugh, the pressures of life fade, and
we feel restored and rejuvenated.

# DAY 2

## *Live Longer Through Laughter*

*Key Truth*

Having a sense of humor
is good for your health.

A friend of mine had a good-humored grandmother who lived to be 103 years old. She was so much fun her family called her "the World's Oldest Living Smart-Aleck." When she went into the hospital at the age of one hundred, my friend called and asked her what was wrong.

"Well, so far they've ruled out pregnancy," she said.

I met someone just like her in our church visitors' line a few years ago. She was a very healthy and sharp ninety-six-year-old lady. Her skin was beautiful. Her eyes were bright. But what struck me most was how happy she was.

It appeared she'd never met a stranger. Everyone around her was her best friend. She was hugging all the people in the line. She was wearing a bright, colorful dress and was a breath of fresh air. After we talked, I hugged her. As I was leaving, I just said in passing, "I believe when I'm ninety-six years old I'm going to look just like you."

She leaned over and whispered in my ear, "Just don't wear the dress."

I thought, *No wonder she's so healthy. She still has a sense of humor. She still knows how to laugh.*

Her good humor was like a healing light flowing through her body. I want to follow her example as I grow older. I've made up my mind that I'll never be a grumpy old man. I will not let myself grow more and more sour the older I become. I'm staying full of joy. When it's my time to go, I'm leaving with a smile on my face, a laugh in my heart, and a joke in my pocket.

## Consider This

Every time you laugh, you reduce the stress hormone and increase production of the human growth hormone, also known as the "youth hormone," by 87 percent. That's the hormone that slows down the aging process and keeps you looking younger and fresher. I laugh all the time, and I don't look seventy-seven years old, do I?

_____

_____

_____

_____

_____

_____

Happiness often sneaks in through a door you didn't know you left open.

—John Barrymore

_____

_____

_____

_____

_____

_____

_____

_____

_____

## What the Scriptures Say

Let the peace of Christ rule in your hearts, since as members of one body you were called to peace. And be thankful.

—Colossians 3:15 (NIV)

Glory in his holy name; let the hearts of those who seek the LORD rejoice.

—1 Chronicles 16:10 (NIV)

## A Prayer for Today

Father, I trust that You have a good plan for me, and I know I can laugh in the days to come. Let my joy be contagious to all who hear me today.

_____

_____

_____

_____

_____

_____

_____

_____

People take different roads seeking fulfillment and happiness. Just because they're not on your road doesn't mean they've gotten lost.

—H. Jackson Browne

_____

_____

_____

_____

_____

_____

_____

### Takeaway Truth

A study said that one of the traits shared
by those who live into their nineties is that
they find joy in everyday life. No doubt
about it, laughter keeps you young.

# DAY 3

## *Pray and Play*

*Key Truth*

Playing, like praying, is good for mind,
body, and soul.

Dr. Stuart Brown, a psychiatrist, is the founder of the National Institute of Play. He became interested in the effects of laughter and play in our lives when the governor of Texas asked him to investigate the tower shootings on the University of Texas campus in 1966. As he studied the life of the troubled young man who had killed sixteen people and wounded thirty-two others, one thing that stuck out was that this young man had never played normally as a child.

He grew up in such a dysfunctional, high-stress family that his "play life" was very limited as a child. This so interested Dr. Brown that he went on to interview other death-row inmates. He discovered that a high percentage of them also had not played normally or freely as children.

Dr. Brown feels that the opposite of play isn't work. It's depression. He believes we need play as much as we need sleep if we want to be physically and emotionally healthy.

With so much sickness and sadness in the world today, I don't know why people don't tap into the healing power of laughter more. It's a free cure with no side effects. You can take it as often as you'd like. I'm no doctor, but I'll write you a prescription today.

Here it is: At least three times a day, every day, take a strong dose of humor. Find something funny that makes you laugh out loud. No chuckling. No laughing on the inside. Trigger those endorphins. Release that joy into the universe so everyone can hear it.

We see this in the Bible, too. After the birth of Isaac, whose name actually means laughter, Sarah was so full of the joy of the Lord that she just had to laugh aloud! What looked impossible with man became possible with God.

Whatever your circumstances may be today, God wants to make you laugh. He wants to fill you with joy knowing that He has victory in store for you. Maybe you're sick and you know God has told you you're going to be well. Or you're struggling financially, but God is saying He's going to prosper you. Perhaps your family is pulled apart. God is saying He's going to bring them back together. Don't listen to negative, self-defeating thoughts. Instead, no matter how you may feel, no matter how bad it looks, let out the laugh of faith and just say, "Ha, ha! I've got inside information. I know God has already worked it out. He's already arranged things in my favor. It's just a matter of time before these promises come to pass."

## Consider This

Medical science tells us that laughing boosts our immune systems. Laughter reduces blood pressure. People who laugh regularly are 40 percent less likely to have a heart attack than those who don't.

_____

_____

_____

_____

_____

_____

_____

People tend to forget that play is serious.

—David Hockney

_____

_____

_____

_____

_____

_____

_____

## What the Scriptures Say

A happy heart is good medicine and a cheerful mind works healing, but a broken spirit dries up the bones.

—Proverbs 17:22 (AMP)

The thief's purpose is to steal and kill and destroy. My purpose is to give them a rich and satisfying life.

—John 10:10 (NLT)

## A Prayer for Today

Father, thank You for making my faith strong and my life rich with joy and laughter.

_____

_____

_____

_____

_____

_____

_____

_____

_____

Play is often talked about as if it were a relief from serious learning. But for children play is serious learning.

—Mr. Rogers

_____

_____

_____

_____

_____

_____

_____

*Takeaway Truth*

Taking time to laugh and play is like taking
vitamins or good medicine.

# A Daily Dose of Humor Works Wonders

*Key Truth*

Those who laugh regularly boost their immune
systems.

When my mother was diagnosed with terminal cancer in 1981,
she was in pain and worried, but instead of staying in bed feeling
sorry for herself, she watched cartoons on television for part of each
day. She would sit there and laugh and laugh despite all she was going
through.

My wise mother was releasing the healing God put on the inside.
If she couldn't find something funny to watch, she'd just go look at
my brother, Paul. That always made her laugh. In case you missed it,
my mother is still laughing today. Doctors had given her only a few
months to live, but more than thirty years later she is cancer-free.
That's the miracle of faith with a healthy dose of laughter.

Our immune systems are made up of millions of cells. The only
purpose for some of these cells is to attack and kill anything foreign
to the body. They're called "NK" or "natural killer" cells. They're
responsible for searching out certain harmful bacteria and viruses
and destroying them. One of their main functions is to attack the
cells that commonly cause cancer.

Researchers have found that every person develops these abnormal cancerous cells on a regular basis. Our natural killer cells usually go to work and make sure they are destroyed. But negative emotions like stress, worry, fear, anxiety, and depression weaken the natural killer cells.

Studies have shown that those who are happy and laugh regularly not only develop more of these natural killer cells than the average person, but the cells' activity is increased.

A doctor friend told me about a woman with a severe case of fibromyalgia. This disorder of unknown origins causes widespread and chronic pain throughout the body. This poor woman spent many hours in bed suffering. She also had chronic fatigue and was very depressed.

Her doctor treated the pain with medications, but he felt the pills were treating only the symptoms and not the cause. In talking to her, the doctor realized how depressed she was. Then he asked her an interesting question: "How long has it been since you've had a good, hearty laugh?"

The lady had to think about it a moment.

"Doctor," she said, "I haven't laughed that way in more than thirty years, since I was a child."

"Well, here's your prescription," he said. "Go watch every funny movie you can find. Go read every funny book you can get your hands on, and laugh as much as you possibly can."

She followed his prescription and little by little, her joy returned. The pain subsided. Her energy was restored. Three months later she returned to the doctor for a checkup. The moment she walked in, he could see the difference. There was a sparkle in her eye, a spring in her step, and a smile on her face.

"Doctor," she said. "I've never felt so good in all my life."

In the months that followed, she continued to laugh more and more. Her laughter cleansed her body of whatever was causing her pain.

## Consider This

When you are good-natured and you see the humor in life, your natural immune system operates at a higher level.

---
---
---
---
---
---
---

The most valuable thing the Psalms do for me is to express the same delight in God which made David dance.

—C. S. Lewis

---
---
---
---
---
---
---
---

## What the Scriptures Say

Beloved, I pray that you may prosper in all things and be in health, just as your soul prospers.

—3 John 2 (NKJV)

"For I know the plans I have for you," declares the LORD, "plans to prosper you and not to harm you, plans to give you hope and a future."

—Jeremiah 29:11 (NIV)

## A Prayer for Today

Father, thank You for the gift of laughter. Help me to see the joy in all circumstances so I can receive Your inner healing. Show me ways to help those around me so together we can live in Your joy and strength.

_____

_____

_____

_____

_____

_____

_____

_____

A good laugh and a long sleep are the best cures in the doctor's book.

—Irish Proverb

_____

_____

_____

_____

_____

_____

_____

_____

_____

*Takeaway Truth*

Laughing and finding happiness in each
day helps boost your body's natural
immune system.

# DAY 5

## *Activate Your Joy*

*Key Truth*
A sense of humor draws people
to you and increases your ability
to deal with life's challenges.

These days you hear constant reports of doom and gloom. More trouble in the economy. Higher taxes. A soaring deficit. Home foreclosures. A tight job market. If you are not careful, you can fall into a trap of thinking, *This is no time to enjoy my life. This is certainly no time to laugh, no time to have a sense of humor.* But in hard times, more than ever, activate your joy. In fact, Job 5:22 says, "You shall laugh at destruction and famine" (NKJV). At first that may not seem to make sense. We're supposed to laugh at famine? We're supposed to laugh at destruction?

Yes, that's exactly right, because in tough times you run a greater risk of losing your joy, so consciously keep your good humor and optimism up in the worst of times. If you become depressed, your brain shuts down, you lose your creativity, and you isolate yourself from friends and family. But the darkest days are when you need all of those assets the most.

Being joyful by laughing and enjoying even the small things reduces the effects of stress, increases brain activity, and heightens creativity, all of which can help you overcome your challenges in difficult times. We use the left side of the brain in most situations, but when we laugh we light up the right side. Research shows that people who've been struggling with a problem and feel stuck tend to do much better if they take a break and enjoy a good laugh. The experts say that without laughter, our thought processes can become stuck, our focus narrows and our ability to solve problems is limited.

The bottom line is this: If you have a sense of humor and you laugh regularly, your mind lights up. You come up with fresh ideas and make better decisions. As a result, your problem-solving abilities are increased.

Sometimes, especially as leaders and as parents, we think being serious and solemn shows our maturity. We want to set a good example at home and at the office. We want to be responsible role models, but being serious all the time isn't good for us or for those who look up to us. Sure, there are times that call for being serious and focused, but there are also times when we need to lighten up, to demonstrate that we can handle pressure and stay in good humor so that creative solutions can be found.

## Consider This

Laughter and good humor offer a common denominator and a shared language. They build bonds that draw people to you and help create mutually supportive networks.

_____

_____

_____

_____

_____

_____

_____

_____

Humor is the great thing, the saving thing. The minute it crops up, all our irritation and resentments slip away, and a sunny spirit takes their place.

—Mark Twain

_____

_____

_____

_____

_____

_____

_____

## What the Scriptures Say

Consider the joy of those corrected by God!
>Do not despise the discipline of the Almighty when you sin.
For though he wounds, he also bandages.
>He strikes, but his hands also heal.
From six disasters he will rescue you;
>even in the seventh, he will keep you from evil.
He will save you from death in time of famine,
>from the power of the sword in time of war.
You will be safe from slander
>and have no fear when destruction comes.
You will laugh at destruction and famine;
>wild animals will not terrify you.
You will be at peace with the stones of the field,
>and its wild animals will be at peace with you.
You will know that your home is safe.
>When you survey your possessions, nothing will be missing.
You will have many children;
>your descendants will be as plentiful as grass!

You will go to the grave at a ripe old age,
>    like a sheaf of grain harvested at the proper time!
"We have studied life and found all this to be true.
>    Listen to my counsel, and apply it to yourself."

>                                        —Job 5:17–27 (NLT)

Dear brothers and sisters, I close my letter with these last words: Be joyful. Grow to maturity. Encourage each other. Live in harmony and peace. Then the God of love and peace will be with you.

>                                  —2 Corinthians 13:11 (NLT)

## A Prayer for Today

Father, give me opportunities today to share Your joy and love with the people around me.

_____

_____

_____

_____

_____

_____

_____

Humor is emotional chaos remembered in tranquility.

>                                        —James Thurber

_____

_____

_____

_____

_____

_____

_____

_____

_____

* * * * * * * * * * * * * * * * * * * * * * * * * * * * * *

### Takeaway Truth

I will take the opportunity to share a laugh with
others each day because laughter helps create
bonds, increases creativity, and enhances my
ability to solve problems.

* * * * * * * * * * * * * * * * * * * * * * * * * * * * * *

## DAY 6

## *Humor Attracts God's Favor*

*Key Truth*

When you bless others with your good humor,
God brings blessings your way.

I recently met an older man who appeared to be in his seventies. I was surprised when he told me he was 106 years old. It wasn't just his unlined face or healthy appearance that threw me off. He was just so happy, so mentally sharp, and so engaged with everyone around him. He stood in the line nearly forty minutes waiting to visit with me. I told him we could have pulled up a chair for him so he would not have had to stand.

"I don't need to sit down," he said. "When I grow old, I'll sit down."

He was a good-natured, handsome African American fellow.

"I can't believe you're 106. You don't have a wrinkle on your face," I said.

"Joel," he replied, "black don't crack."

Then he ran off two or three more jokes. We laughed and laughed. I normally don't like it when someone in my church has better jokes than me, but I forgave him.

When he walked away, he turned around and said to everyone, "I'll see you next year."

I had no doubt that God would reward him with another year because he was spreading so much joy everywhere he went. I thought to myself that it was no wonder he seemed so healthy; he was so full of joy. He had a great sense of humor. He loved to laugh. Think about all of God's natural healing that had been released and flowing in him all these years.

Sometimes we think the older we are, the more somber we should be and the less fun we should have. But I don't believe that's God's plan. If you don't have joy, laugh regularly, and take the time to play, you will not finish life the way God wants you to finish.

One of the things about the 106-year-old man that struck me was that he enjoyed poking fun at himself and his advanced age. He saw the humor in growing old, and he laughed at the same things that might frustrate others in their later years. Being willing to laugh at yourself and at life's ups and downs may be one of the greatest gifts you can have.

## Consider This

We've all known people who throw fits when they make mistakes. Some throw golf clubs. Others throw their bats and helmets. A few throw punches. How much fun are they to be around? But the person who laughs at mistakes, flubs, and goofs is someone people want to share their time with.

_____

_____

_____

_____

_____

_____

_____

_____

A kind heart is a fountain of gladness, making everything in its vicinity freshen into smiles.

—Washington Irving

---
---
---
---
---
---
---

## What the Scriptures Say

Sing, O heavens; and be joyful, O earth; and break forth into singing, O mountains: for the LORD hath comforted his people, and will have mercy upon his afflicted.

—Isaiah 49:13 (KJV)

But none of these things move me; nor do I count my life dear to myself, so that I may finish my race with joy, and the ministry which I received from the Lord Jesus, to testify to the gospel of the grace of God.

—Acts 20:24 (NKJV)

## A Prayer for Today

Father, thank You for doing a work in my life. Thank You for molding me and shaping me into Your image. I ask for Your supernatural joy and strength to stand strong no matter what I face.

---
---

_____

_____

_____

_____

_____

_____

_____

A person without a sense of humor is like a wagon without springs—jolted by every pebble in the road.

—Henry Ward Beecher

_____

_____

_____

_____

_____

_____

_____

_____

### Takeaway Truth

God rewards those who reflect His goodness
and make the world a more welcoming place.
You and all those around you will benefit from
your laughter and good humor, so feel free to
share it every day at every opportunity.

# The Family That Laughs Together Stays Together

*Key Truth*

Family bonds grow stronger
through shared laughter.

A few years ago, right before I stepped up onto the platform to minister, Victoria told me that my hair was sticking up in the back.

"Put a little hair spray back there," my wife said.

I didn't know where the hair spray was.

"It's back in the bathroom, on the shelf, in a red can."

I was in a big hurry so I hustled back and grabbed the red can off the shelf. Then I sprayed and sprayed that little sprig of stand-up hair, but it would not stay down. So I sprayed it a couple more times and headed out the door.

After the service that day, Victoria said, "Why didn't you spray your hair? It was still sticking up."

"Victoria, I did spray. But that hair spray you gave me doesn't work. I sprayed and sprayed."

She then kindly offered to show me how to use hair spray. I brought the red can out and handed it to her.

She studied it for a second and then broke up laughing.

"Joel, this isn't hair spray. This is air freshener."

I just smiled and said, "You know what? Even if it does stick up, I've got the best smelling hair around."

We've established that smiling regularly and having a sense of humor improve your health and attract others, so for the last twenty-four years I've been keeping Victoria happy and surrounded by friendly people. Sometimes, I make her laugh without even trying. That's a good thing because research has also shown that the couples and families who laugh together stay together. They have stronger relationships and tighter bonds. As you might suspect, we are a very tight family.

## Consider This

Laughter is a great addition to every home. The enemy cannot stand the sound of joyful laughing. He cannot stand the sound of husbands and wives and family members having fun together. He wants there to be so much strife, tension, and pressure that we never have any joy in our homes. We all need to laugh together and stay in good humor to keep from falling into that trap.

_____

_____

_____

_____

_____

_____

_____

I think the next best thing to solving a problem is finding some humor in it.

—Frank A. Clark

_____

_____

_____

_____

_____

_____

_____

_____

## What the Scriptures Say

Delight yourself also in the Lord, and He will give you the desires and secret petitions of your heart.

—Psalm 37:4 (AMP)

Please don't squander one bit of this marvelous life God has given us.

—2 Corinthians 6:1 (The Message)

## A Prayer for Today

Father, thank You for the precious gift of laughter today. Help me to be a blessing to others so I can make the most of every moment. I bless You and thank You for the good plan You have for me.

_____

_____

_____

_____

_____

_____

_____

_____

_____

When you look at your life, the greatest happinesses are family happinesses.

—Joyce Brothers

_____

_____

_____

_____

_____

_____

_____

_____

### Takeaway Truth
Families who laugh together are better equipped
to face adversity and deal with life's challenges,
so encourage laughter and joy in your home.

# STEP SIX

....................

## *Be a Dream Releaser*

# DAY 1

## *Use Your Influence to Help Others*

. . . . . . . . . . . . . . . . . . . . . . . . . . . . . . . . . . . . . . . . . . . .

### *Key Truth*
You will always have what you want if you help
others get what they want.

. . . . . . . . . . . . . . . . . . . . . . . . . . . . . . . . . . . . . . . . . . . .

Cheryl, who works at a big corporation, told me that her supervisor refused to train her on a new computer program. The company had sent this supervisor to a class so she could learn how to run the program, but when she came back she wouldn't share any of the information. She was afraid if she helped others, they might get promoted over her. So she kept the knowledge and training to herself.

But the truth is, when you hold others back, you are really holding yourself back. If you will live unselfishly and help others reach your level, God will make sure somebody is there to lift you higher, too. Alec, a professional mountain climber, was on his way to the top of a peak when a snowstorm hit. It was very cold and hard to breathe. Even some of the most experienced mountain climbers couldn't make it.

A little farther up the mountain, the storm turned into a blizzard. They were still six hours from the top. Climbing was extremely difficult. Each step was a struggle. Then, Alec saw another climber lying along the trail curled up, asleep or passed out. He was in danger of freezing to death. He had a faint heartbeat and was barely strong enough to breathe.

Several other climbers had passed by. Alec's team told him to keep going.

"If you stop and try to help him, you could lose your own life," they said.

Alec could not leave him there to die. He told the team to go on. Alec knelt beside the fallen climber. He massaged the man's arms and legs and face to get the blood flowing and keep him awake. His efforts revived the stricken man enough that Alec was able to get him on his feet and walk him down the mountain, saving his life.

The doctor who examined them both told Alec that he'd done more than save a life. He'd likely saved two.

"Your arms and legs show early signs of frostbite," the doctor said. "You wouldn't have made it much higher before you'd have been in serious trouble yourself. Your efforts to save the fallen climber probably benefited you as much as him because it increased your circulation and forced you to head down the mountain."

It's easy to get so caught up in your climb to the top that you don't want to stop and help someone else. But when you take time to help others in their struggles, you set yourself up for even greater victories.

The apostle Paul would never have become such a major figure of faith without the support of another disciple, Barnabas. As you may know, Paul was not always a believer. In fact, he'd once been known as Saul, a persecutor of believers.

Saul's attitude changed dramatically on the road to Damascus when God touched his life and transformed him into the apostle Paul we all know and love.

But it took awhile for the apostle Paul to convince the other followers of Jesus that he wasn't the same old Saul. In Acts 9:26, we are told of this fear and suspicion toward the new apostle.

The next verse says that Barnabas stood up for Paul. Barnabas put in a good word for him. He said, in effect, "Hey, I can vouch for Paul. I know who he is. He is the real deal."

If it had not been for Barnabas using his influence, Paul probably would not have been in a position to write more than half of the New

Testament. We don't hear a lot about Barnabas. Paul greatly overshadowed him. But if you were to talk to Paul, he would say, "I succeeded because Barnabas dared to take a risk and opened a door that I could not open on my own. Barnabas believed in me when nobody else did."

Even more powerful is the fact that every life Paul touched later would mean a reward for Barnabas as well. There is no greater legacy than to help someone else win.

## Consider This

When you help others to succeed, you are sowing a seed for yourself to rise higher.

_____

_____

_____

_____

_____

_____

_____

One thing I know; the only ones among you who will be really happy are those who will have sought and found how to serve.
—Albert Schweitzer

_____

_____

_____

_____

_____

_____

_____

## What the Scriptures Say

When Saul arrived in Jerusalem, he tried to meet with the believers, but they were all afraid of him. They did not believe he had truly become a believer! Then Barnabas brought him to the apostles and told them how Saul had seen the Lord on the way to Damascus and how the Lord had spoken to Saul. He also told them that Saul had preached boldly in the name of Jesus in Damascus.

So Saul stayed with the apostles and went all around Jerusalem with them, preaching boldly in the name of the Lord. He debated with some Greek-speaking Jews, but they tried to murder him. When the believers heard about this, they took him down to Caesarea and sent him away to Tarsus, his hometown.

The church then had peace throughout Judea, Galilee, and Samaria, and it became stronger as the believers lived in the fear of the Lord. And with the encouragement of the Holy Spirit, it also grew in numbers.

—Acts 9:26–31 (NLT)

All the promises of God in Him are Yes, and in Him Amen, to the glory of God through us.

—2 Corinthians 1:20 (NKJV)

## A Prayer for Today

Father, thank You for Your truth, which sets me free today. It is my delight to do Your will and help others succeed. Show me ways to be a blessing and help others. Let everything I do bring glory to You.

_____

_____

_____

_____

_____

_____

_____

_____

Do all the good you can, by all the means you can,
In all the ways you can, in all the places you can,
To all the people you can, as long as ever you can.

—John Wesley

_____

_____

_____

_____

_____

_____

_____

### Takeaway Truth

If you want to be happy and joyful, use your
influence to help others succeed. Take time to
give good advice. Introduce others to helpful
people you know. Make a phone call and put
in a good word whenever possible. When you
help others win, God will make sure you are
surrounded by people who will help you
win in return.

# Lend a Hand to God Himself

*Key Truth*
One key to happiness is to
serve others gladly.

A letter came to me early in my days as pastor of our church. I'd stepped onto the platform after my father's passing but still didn't feel at home taking his place. I was very unsure of myself on Sunday mornings. I found the envelope on my desk during that period of self-doubt, and when I saw the name on the return address I recognized it immediately.

It was from John Maxwell, a former pastor and best-selling author. I had never met him, but I had admired his writing and teachings. I opened that letter as quickly as I could, and then I was touched by what he'd written.

"I watched you on television on Sunday and you were outstanding," he wrote. "I've got to tell you, you've got what it takes."

In the letter he went on to list several things that he liked about my talk. "You keep it simple," he wrote. "You've got a good personality." He also offered several suggestions: "Here's some advice. Here's what you can do to be less nervous. Here's what I do when I'm preparing."

John Maxwell was sharing his secrets. Giving his encouragement. He had forty years of experience, and he was voluntarily pouring it into a young man he'd never even met before. He didn't have to do that. He'd already reached a high level of accomplishment. He'd won his place of respect. But John understands this principle: True success is when you reach back and bring somebody along with you.

I arranged to meet with John a few weeks after I received his note, which I still have. Because of what he did for me, John will be a friend of mine for life. He spoke encouragement into me at a very critical time on my journey.

Who has God put in your life like this man placed in mine? Supportive and encouraging people don't show up in your life by accident. God brings such people across our paths on purpose. We each should live with this awareness: *I am here to add value to people. I am here to help others succeed.*

When we love and serve others, putting their needs above our own, we are honoring Him. When we carry one another's burdens, we are fulfilling the law of Christ, which is to love others.

There are many ways to reach out to people and help shoulder their loads. Sharing an encouraging word or smile, praying and interceding, offering guidance in your area of expertise, or even just paying for someone's groceries or tank of gas can make a difference. Anytime you help others and reach out to those in need, Scripture says you are directly lending a hand to God Himself.

## Consider This

Don't go around thinking, *I wonder what they can do for me? I wonder what they have to offer?* Your attitude should be to think of what helping hand you can offer others, what you can teach them, and what connections you can share. Like John Maxwell, look for opportunities to call out the seeds of greatness God has planted in each of us.

_____

_____

_____

_____

_____

_____

_____

_____

_____

Find out how much God has given you and from it take what you need; the remainder is needed by others.

—Saint Augustine

_____

_____

_____

_____

_____

_____

_____

_____

_____

## What the Scriptures Say

Carry each other's burdens, and in this way you will fulfill the law of Christ.

—Galatians 6:2 (NIV)

As each has received a gift, use it to serve one another, as good stewards of God's varied grace.

—1 Peter 4:10 (ESV)

## A Prayer for Today

Father, I want to fulfill Your law of love by serving and helping others. Show me how to be a blessing to the people around me so that I can help carry their burdens.

_____

_____

_____

_____

_____

_____

_____

_____

Everybody can be great. Because anybody can serve. You don't have to have a college degree to serve. You don't have to make your subject and your verb agree to serve.... You don't have to know the second theory of thermodynamics in physics to serve. You only need a heart full of grace. A soul generated by love.

—Martin Luther King, Jr.

_____

_____

_____

_____

_____

_____

_____

_____

### Takeaway Truth

Today, look for ways to lighten the load for the people around you. Be a burden-lifter. Remember, in God's kingdom, what you sow, you shall reap. When you help others, God promises to repay you. He'll pour out His victory and blessing upon you all the days of your life!

# DAY 3

## *Invest in the Success of Others*

*Key Truth*
Learn to believe in people
before they succeed.

. . . . . . . . . . . . . . . . . . . . . . . . . . . . . . . . . . . . . . . . . . .

I have a friend who is black and grew up in poverty in a housing project. His mother raised him on her own. His future looked bleak, even though he was very bright. But he worked hard, and with God's favor he earned a scholarship to an Ivy League college.

Most of his fellow students were from white, well-to-do families. His roommate was a sharp young white man from an upper-income family who had traveled the world. My friend had rarely left his neighborhood. Their lives were very different, yet they became best friends. He told his roommate that his dream was to become a television news journalist. He'd dreamed of that job since childhood.

His roommate supported him but said, "You'll never become a journalist with your vocabulary like it is. It's too limited. We've got to do something about it." The roommate saw his potential and invested in it. They worked on his vocabulary together, studying the dictionary and practicing pronunciation.

This went on day after day, week after week. For four years the roommate taught my friend a new word every day. The roommate was a dream releaser. He'd been blessed with a good upbringing and far more resources. Now, he passed on the blessings, investing in the success of another person from a far less privileged background.

Today that young man from the projects, Byron Pitts, is an award-winning journalist seen by millions of people every week on *60 Minutes*, the number one news program in America. He told me, "I would never be where I am if it were not for my roommate. I would have never made it this far if he had not taken time to invest in me."

Anybody can be a friend after someone is successful, after they win, after they are promoted, after they break the addiction. But when they need us the most is before they are successful.

Many people need only a little help, a bit of advice, a word of encouragement. Do for them what you would want somebody to do for you. You may have experiences that could save others heartache and pain. Don't keep your knowledge to yourself. Pick up the phone. Call them. Help someone grow into greatness.

When you help others succeed, you will find abundant success on your path, too. What are you investing in the lives of the people around you? Are you helping others get ahead? There are people in your life who hold the keys for you to reach your full potential. These are people whom God has placed in your life for you to help along. The higher they rise up, the higher you will rise up.

If you want God's continued blessing on your life, you can't be selfish. You must go out of your way to help others. You must make some sacrifices, to teach, to train, to share what you know to help others find their happiness and joy.

## Consider This

God's system works on the principle of sowing and reaping. What you pour out will come back to you in increased measure. When you give generously, a generous harvest will return to you.

_____

_____

_____

_____

_____

_____

My piece of bread only belongs to me when I know that everyone else has a share, and that no one starves while I eat.

—Leo Tolstoy

_____

_____

_____

_____

_____

_____

_____

_____

## What the Scriptures Say

Do you see someone skilled in their work? They will serve
before kings.

—Proverbs 22:29 (NIV)

Send your grain across the seas, and in time, profits will flow
back to you.

—Ecclesiastes 11:1 (NLT)

## A Prayer for Today

Father in heaven, I open my heart to Your heart. I invite You to use me to be a blessing in the lives of others. Show me where to invest my time, talent, and resources for Your glory.

_____

_____

_____

_____

_____

_____

_____

_____

_____

I've learned that you shouldn't go through life with a catcher's mitt on both hands. You need to be able to throw something back.

—Maya Angelou

_____

_____

_____

_____

_____

_____

_____

_____

_____

_____

*Takeaway Truth*

When you give generously of your time, talent, and resources, you are setting yourself up for greater success. People will come across your path who will help you grow and reach your full potential. But you have to do your part by stepping out and sowing the seed. Be on the lookout for ways you can help others. As you give of yourself to help others grow, you'll rise higher and live the abundant life God has in store for you.

## DAY 4

# Be a People Builder

*Key Truth*

When you give to others without asking for anything in return, you build them up while also creating your own support base.

Helen, a junior high math teacher in Minnesota, spent most of the school week teaching a difficult "new math" lesson. She could tell her students were frustrated and restless by week's end. They were becoming rowdy, so she told them to put their books away. She then instructed the class to take out clean sheets of paper. She gave each of them this assignment: Write down every one of your classmates' names on the left, and then, on the right, put down one thing you like about that student.

The tense and rowdy mood subsided and the room quieted when the students went to work. Their moods lifted as they dug into the assignment. There was frequent laughter and giggling. They looked around the room, sharing quips about one another. Helen's class was a much happier group when the bell signaled the end of the school day.

She took their lists home over the weekend and spent both days off recording what was said about each student on separate sheets of paper so she could pass on all the nice things said about each person without giving away who said what.

The next Monday she handed out the lists she'd made for each student. The room buzzed with excitement and laughter.

"Wow. Thanks! This is the coolest!"

"I didn't think anyone even noticed me!"

"Someone thinks I'm beautiful?"

Helen had come up with the exercise just to settle down her class, but it ended up giving them a big boost. They grew closer as classmates and more confident as individuals. She could tell they all seemed more relaxed and joyful.

About ten years later, Helen learned that one of her favorite students in that class, a charming boy named Mark, had been killed while serving in Vietnam. She received an invitation to the funeral from Mark's parents, who included a note saying they wanted to be sure she came to their farmhouse after the services to speak with them.

Helen arrived and the grieving parents took her aside. The father showed her Mark's billfold, and then from it he removed two worn pieces of lined paper that had been taped, folded, and refolded many times over the years. Helen recognized her handwriting on the paper and tears came to her eyes.

Mark's parents said he'd always carried the list of nice things written by his classmates. "Thank you so much for doing that," his mother said. "He treasured it, as you can see."

Still teary-eyed, Helen walked into the kitchen where many of Mark's former junior high classmates were assembled. They saw that Mark's parents had his list from that class. One by one, they either produced their own copies from wallets and purses or they confessed to keeping their lists in an album, drawer, diary, or file at home.

Helen the teacher was a "people builder." She instinctively found ways to build up her students. Being a people builder means you consistently find ways to invest in and bring out the best in others. You give without asking for anything in return. You offer advice, speak faith into them, build their confidence, and challenge them to go higher.

God designed us to live in relationship with others. He wants us to help each other grow. We need people in our lives to encourage us, and we need to encourage the people in our lives and help them reach their potential. The word *encourage* means "to urge forward." Many times you can see things in other people that they don't see themselves. You can see their strengths and talents. You can see that God has a special plan for them, even though they may be going through a difficult time.

Don't assume that people see what you see in them. Take a moment and encourage them with either a kind word or a simple note. There might be a special gift you can give that will remind them of their goal or dream. In whatever way you can, urge the people in your life to keep moving forward. If you'll be a people builder and help others fulfill their dreams, God will help you fulfill your dreams also, and you'll live in blessing all the days of your life.

## Consider This

All most people need is a boost to help them help themselves; a little encouragement to become what God created them to be.

_____

_____

_____

_____

_____

_____

_____

The true meaning of life is to plant trees, under whose shade you do not expect to sit.

—Nelson Henderson

_____

_____

_____

_____

_____

_____

_____

## What the Scriptures Say

The Son of Man came not to be served but to serve, and to give his life as a ransom for many.

—Matthew 20:28 (ESV)

Encourage one another and build each other up.

—I Thessalonians 5:11 (NIV)

## A Prayer for Today

Father, thank You for the people You have placed in my life. Help me build them up and find creative ways to urge them forward to Your glory.

_____

_____

_____

_____

_____

_____

This is the true joy in life—being used for a purpose recognized by yourself as a mighty one; being thoroughly worn out before you are thrown on the scrap heap; being a force of nature instead of a feverish selfish little clod of ailments and grievances complaining that the world will not devote itself to making you happy.

—George Bernard Shaw

_____

_____

_____

_____

_____

_____

_____

### Takeaway Truth

None of us will reach our highest potential without help from others. We need one another. You can be the one to tip the scales for someone else. You can be the one to stir up their seeds of greatness by reaching out to them, encouraging them, and offering help without asking for anything in return.

# DAY 5

## *Offer Words of Encouragement*

*Key Truth*

You have the ability to stir someone's dreams by
giving them permission to succeed.

M y friend Robert told me about an uncle who set him on a path
to success early in life. This uncle had been in China since his birth,
but when he returned they met on the front porch of the Iowa farm
where Robert grew up.

He'd watched the uncle's car driving toward the family's home on
their dusty lane, and Robert was so excited to finally meet this uncle.
When he pulled in the gate little Robert ran out there to meet him.
The uncle got out, gave him a big hug, and swung him around and
around.

"You must be Robert. I've heard so much about you," the uncle said.

Then the uncle stepped back and looked at him. And out of the
blue he said, "You know what, Robert? I think one day you're going
to be a minister. In fact, I think one day you're going to be a great
minister."

Why did the uncle say this? There were no ministers in this family. He simply felt something inside, and he was bold enough to speak
it out by faith. He planted a seed in little Robert's heart. That night as
Robert lay in his bed he secretly prayed, "God, let what my uncle said
be true. Let me be a minister one day."

As you may know, Robert Schuller, who grew up in Alton, Iowa, became one of the great ministers of our time. Isn't it amazing what a simple word of encouragement can do? Look what it did in his life.

You can light a fire on the inside that glows joyfully for a lifetime. When you take time to believe in someone, and you speak faith into the heart of another, your words can become the seed God nourishes.

I'm asking you to grant others the permission to succeed. Be a seed planter. I know an older gentleman who is great at this. Any time he sees a small child, he'll ask the parents' permission to call them over and say, "Young man (or Young lady), I have a very special talent, something only a few people can do. I have the ability to pick a winner."

The child's eyes usually grow big. He'll ask the child if he can do an evaluation. Of course, the parents are playing along. He'll stand back and look at the child, and walk around very slowly, saying, "Uh-huh. Yes. Okay. I see..."

When he finishes the "evaluation," he'll say, "I have great news. I've never been wrong. I'm right every time. You, my friend, indeed, you are a winner!"

The child lights up with a smile, runs back to the parents, and says, "Hey, Mom. Hey, Dad. Guess what? I'm a winner."

My friend is building up those children, urging them forward, bolstering their confidence, and instilling self-esteem.

This is such a simple thing to do, yet so many people benefit. I'm sure there are many in your life—people you work with, play sports with, and live near—who could use an encouraging and approving word. Someone around you is craving your blessing.

## Consider This

You can't imagine what it will mean to those you affirm when you give them your approval. Let them know in no uncertain terms that you are proud of them and you think they are destined to do great things. Everyone needs to be valued. Everyone needs to be appreciated. Every person needs that blessing.

_____

_____

_____

_____

_____

_____

_____

_____

Let us have faith that right makes might; and, let us to the end
dare to do our duty.

—Abraham Lincoln

_____

_____

_____

_____

_____

_____

_____

_____

## What the Scriptures Say

You are the salt of the earth, but if salt has lost its taste, how
shall its saltiness be restored? It is no longer good for anything
except to be thrown out and trampled under people's feet. You
are the light of the world. A city set on a hill cannot be hidden.
Nor do people light a lamp and put it under a basket, but on a
stand, and it gives light to all in the house. In the same way, let

your light shine before others, so that they may see your good works and give glory to your Father who is in heaven.

—Matthew 5:13–16 (ESV)

Give, and it will be given to you. A good measure, pressed down, shaken together and running over, will be poured into your lap.

—Luke 6:38 (NIV)

## A Prayer for Today

Father in heaven, I receive Your Word into my heart today. Thank You for choosing to bless me so that I can be a blessing to others. Show me ways to bless others and teach me to receive all You have for me.

_____

_____

_____

_____

_____

_____

_____

We make a living by what we get, but we make a life by what we give.

—Winston Churchill

_____

_____

_____

_____

_____

_____

_____

_____

_____

### Takeaway Truth

Don't become so focused on your own dreams,
your own goals, that your thinking becomes
in-grown. Be on the lookout for those you can
urge forward. Learn to speak faith into them.
Give them a greater vision. Speak the
blessing over their lives.

# DAY 6

## *We Rise to Expectations*

*Key Truth*

We all need someone to believe in us more than
we believe in ourselves, to see our potential, to
look beyond where we are now and guide us to
what God has planned for us.

Jesus didn't focus on the faults of those around Him. He saw their potential. His disciple Peter, in particular, was rough around the edges, hot-tempered and foulmouthed. Yet Jesus looked beyond all that and saw Peter's potential.

Jesus spoke faith into Peter and helped him form a vision of himself rising higher and overcoming obstacles. His encouragement helped Peter become what he was created to be. Proverbs 12:25 says that a word of encouragement works wonders. When you help people expand their thinking to create a real vision of victory for their lives, they will accomplish things that they never could have before. Their success will come, in part, as the result of your faith, your confidence in them, and the seeds you planted to help them grow.

The principal in a California high school conducted an experiment in which he told three teachers that they'd been judged the brightest and most effective educators in their school district. As a result, they'd been selected for a new program.

"We are giving you the top ninety students, the smartest students with the highest IQs, and you will teach them accelerated courses," the teachers were told.

The students and the teachers naturally were excited and proud to be selected as "the cream of the crop." Their performances improved dramatically in the new program. At the end of that school year, those three classes had learned 30 percent more than the other students. They were 30 percent further along in their educations.

Imagine their shock when the principal informed the teachers that this was only an experiment, and in reality their students had been randomly selected and were not high achievers. Still, the teachers were amazed at how well the students had performed and they congratulated themselves. Then the principal broke the rest of the news.

They were not the top three teachers in the district. They, too, had been randomly selected. The principal's experiment confirmed that we rise to the level of our expectations. When you build up those around you, they rise to your expectations.

## Consider This

You are the cream of the crop. I have incredible confidence in you. I know you will do great things. You will fulfill your God-given destiny, and you will multiply your blessings by encouraging others.

_____

_____

_____

_____

_____

_____

_____

What the teacher is, is more important than what he teaches.
—Karl Menninger

_____
_____
_____
_____
_____
_____
_____

## What the Scriptures Say

That day the LORD exalted Joshua in the sight of all Israel; and they stood in awe of him all the days of his life.

—Joshua 4:14 (NIV)

Arise, shine, for your light has come, and the glory of the LORD rises upon you.

—Isaiah 60:1 (NIV)

## A Prayer for Today

Father, I come to You with an open and humble heart. Thank You for choosing me and for preparing a bright future for me. I will rise and I will shine. Let everything I do bring honor to You.

_____
_____
_____
_____
_____
_____
_____

The first question which the priest and the Levite asked was: "If I stop to help this man, what will happen to me?" But...the good Samaritan reversed the question: "If I do not stop to help this man, what will happen to him?"

—Martin Luther King, Jr.

_____

_____

_____

_____

_____

_____

_____

_____

_____

_____

### Takeaway Truth

Look around and see whom God has put in your life to inspire and motivate. Even small gestures like a kind word, a note of encouragement, or recognizing a person's gifts can make a difference to someone in need of a boost.

# DAY 7

## *Live as a Healer*

*Key Truth*
Just a few kind words can start
the healing process.

. . . . . . . . . . . . . . . . . . . . . . . . . . . . . . . . . . . . . . . . . .

A well-dressed man stopped me on a busy sidewalk not long ago. From his appearance, you'd think he was on top of the world, but behind the facade, he was in much pain. He and his wife had separated. He was so discouraged.

"I don't have a reason to live anymore," he told me.

He sobbed and sobbed. My coat was wet with his tears. I didn't have all the answers. I couldn't solve all of his problems right there on the sidewalk. But I could pour in some healing oil. I offered words of encouragement.

"God has you in the palm of His hand," I said. "Our meeting is not an accident. That's God's way of saying, 'Everything will be all right.'"

It's amazing what happens when you tell someone, "Everything is going to be all right. You're going to make it. There are good days up ahead." That's all some people need to hear. You don't have to preach a sermon. You don't have to quote twenty-five Scripture verses or counsel them for eight hours.

After I prayed with the man on the street, he noticed how wet my suit was from his tears. He was embarrassed. "Oh, Joel. It looks like I've ruined your jacket."

I didn't tell him, but I wore those tears like medals on my jacket. You're never more like God than when you're helping those who are hurting. One of our assignments in life is to help wipe away the tears.

Everywhere we go there are people in need. There may be smiles on the outside, but on the inside there is pain. Many are quietly hurting and they need healing. We all have a ministry. It may not be in the pulpit, but God is counting on each of us to reach out to others and bring healing wherever we go.

Are you sensitive to the needs of those around you? Your friends? Your neighbors? Your co-workers? Many times, like the man who stopped me on the street, someone may be hurting, but they hide it because of shame or embarrassment. Often, they don't know how to reach out for help, so be prepared to reach out to them. Be a healer. Be a restorer. Take time to wipe away the tears.

Your job is not to judge. God wants you to lift the fallen, restore the broken, and heal the hurting.

Too often we focus on our own goals and our own dreams, hoping for a miracle, but I've learned that I can become someone's miracle. There is healing in our hands. There's healing in our voices. We are containers filled with God's love.

You are full of encouragement, mercy, restoration, and healing. Everywhere you go, dispense the goodness of God. You can say to those in need:

- "You may have made mistakes, but God's mercy is bigger than any mistake you've made."
- "You may have wasted years of your life making poor choices, but God still has a way to get you to your final destination."
- "You may have had an addiction, but the power of the Most High God can break any addiction and set you free."

## Consider This

That's what it means to dispense good. You lift the fallen. You encourage the discouraged. You take time to wipe away the tears.

_____

_____

_____

_____

_____

_____

_____

_____

Our prayers for others flow more easily than those for ourselves. This shows we are made to live by charity.

—C. S. Lewis

_____

_____

_____

_____

_____

_____

_____

_____

## What the Scriptures Say

Gentle words are a tree of life.

—Proverbs 15:4 (NLT)

We are therefore Christ's ambassadors, as though God were making his appeal through us.

—2 Corinthians 5:20 (NIV)

## A Prayer for Today

Father God, thank You for choosing me and using me. Once again, I surrender every area of my life to You. Show me ways to be a miracle to others so that my life brings glory to You.

_____

_____

_____

_____

_____

_____

_____

_____

_____

I can think of no more stirring symbol of man's humanity to man than a fire engine.

—Kurt Vonnegut

_____

_____

_____

_____

_____

_____

_____

_____

### Takeaway Truth

Today, you can be someone's miracle. Look for
ways to reach out to people in need. Choose to
be kind, loving, merciful, and understanding.
Use gentle words to bring healing to
those around you!

# STEP SEVEN

......................................

## Celebrate Yourself

# Encourage Yourself by Remembering God's Blessings

*Key Truth*

It's good to have friends and family around to cheer you up when you're down, but in order to truly live in victory, that encouragement has to come from the inside.

When your mind is telling you it's not worth it, when your circumstances seem difficult, deep down inside, call up your victories in the past and think about when God has stepped into your life before. The Bible tells us that's what David had to do. He was facing a major setback. His family was killed, his city was destroyed, and his own people were now against him, but he still managed to encourage himself in the Lord. How did he do that? He replayed in his mind the victories from the past. He recounted God's faithfulness. As he rehearsed over and over the goodness of God, strength began to rise in his heart.

The great football player Emmitt Smith did much the same thing many times in his career. When you look at how successful and celebrated he is today, you might be tempted to think that he never needed to encourage himself. The former Dallas Cowboys running back holds the record for most yards rushing in NFL history. He has three Super Bowl rings. He was inducted into the Pro Football Hall of Fame in 2010. A few years before that, he won the *Dancing with the Stars* competition! And he is also married to a beautiful woman, a former Miss Virginia.

But Emmitt grew up in a low-income family and spent his first few years living in public housing. He made a name for himself as a football player in high school and college. But there were many who thought he'd never make it in the National Football League. Many scouts and coaches felt he was too short at five feet nine inches tall. Others said he wasn't fast enough to play in the pros.

On his NFL draft day, Emmitt waited with his family and friends for his name to be called. But after fifteen others were chosen in the draft, he still had not received a call. Emmitt began to doubt himself. He questioned his decision to leave the University of Florida before his senior year. Nervous and discouraged, he went for a walk on the beach outside a friend's Florida condominium.

As Emmitt walked alone, he didn't let himself think of the fifteen other players who'd been called before him. Instead, he encouraged himself by thinking of all that he'd accomplished so far. In high school, he'd led his football team to two state championships and set the state record for rushing yards. In just three seasons of college football, he'd set fifty-eight school records and was named an All-American.

After raising his spirits by remembering his victories, Emmitt prayed, "God, it's all in Your hands." Then he returned to the condo where everyone was gathered. They informed him that he hadn't been the sixteenth pick in the NFL draft either.

Just then the phone rang. It was Jimmy Johnson, then the coach of the Dallas Cowboys.

"Emmitt, would you like to wear a star on your helmet?" said Coach Johnson.

"Yes, Coach, I would love to wear a Cowboys star," said Emmitt.

Maybe you are discouraged and doubting yourself right now. Maybe you've lost your fire and your enthusiasm because of a disappointment or setback.

Encourage yourself as Emmitt did. Look back on past accomplishments and victories and draw inspiration from them. Stay focused on encouraging thoughts—thoughts of hope and thoughts of faith.

When you're in difficult times and you're tempted to get down—whether it's a bad medical report, a relationship problem, or you are struggling in your finances—don't dwell on the negative and replay over and over all the reasons why things won't work out and how impossible your situation is. Instead, replay in your mind all the times that God helped you, the times God protected you from accidents, and the times God gave you a promotion even though you weren't the most qualified.

## Consider This

Every one of us has seen the hand of God at work in our lives. A key to encouraging yourself is to replay those victories. As you remember the great things God has done, faith will fill your heart. Strength and courage will come from the inside. No matter what you're facing, no matter how difficult it looks, you'll know deep down, *God did not bring me this far to leave me here. If He did it for me in the past, He'll do it again for me in the future.*

_____

_____

_____

_____

_____

_____

_____

_____

Mishaps are like knives, that either serve us or cut us, as we grasp them by the blade or the handle.

—James Russell Lowell

_____

_____

_____

_____

_____

_____

## What the Scriptures Say

David was now in great danger because all his men were very bitter about losing their sons and daughters, and they began to talk of stoning him. But David found strength in the LORD his God.

—1 Samuel 30:6 (NLT)

Do not be anxious about anything, but in everything by prayer and supplication with thanksgiving let your requests be made known to God.

—Philippians 4:6 (ESV)

## A Prayer for Today

Father, thank You for Your faithfulness today. I choose to focus on You and the good things You have prepared for my future. I thank You for making a way out of no way, and I will bless You always.

_____

_____

_____

_____

_____

I have heard there are troubles of more than one kind.
Some come from ahead and some come from behind.
But I've bought a big bat. I'm all ready you see.
Now my troubles are going to have troubles with me!

—Dr. Seuss

### Takeaway Truth

There are so many places you can see the
hand of God at work. Thank Him for saving
you today. Stir up that inner strength and
encouragement. As you do, you'll rise higher
and higher and live the life of victory the
Lord has prepared for you.

# Create an Encouragement File

*Key Truth*
It's okay to encourage yourself because
that's what God did.

Whenever someone sends you a kind note or a compliment, put it in a file in your home or office. Then, when you're tempted to be down, pull out those letters and read them again. Let those words lift your spirits.

I started an Encouragement File when I first began ministering. Whenever someone sent me a kind note, a nice letter, or even when someone just gave me a compliment, I'd put it in the file. Back in those days, if someone said something even halfway encouraging, I put it in there. I remember this elderly man I'd see at the gym was always kidding me about something. But one day he wrote me a note that said, "I watched your sermon on television yesterday. All I can say is, 'Better luck next time.'"

I was so happy that he at least watched the sermon, I put his note in my Encouragement File. Sometimes you can't be picky. Thank God, today his note is in "File 13." I don't need that one anymore.

Shortly after I became a minister, this little boy about five years old came up after my sermon and said: "I really love listening to your stories."

I was feeling so good.

Then he said, "But if I were you, I'd leave out all that other boring stuff."

You need an Encouragement File, too. In my file I have letters, compliments, and birthday cards. Not long ago one of my third-grade teachers wrote my mom a note about what a good student I was, and how friendly I was, and how I smiled so much even back then. That encouraged me. I put my teacher's note in my file. And now, at least every couple of months, I'll pull out that file and flip through some of those letters.

What am I doing? I'm encouraging myself. It's like being on a good maintenance program. Be encouraged on a regular basis.

If you are worried that no one has sent you nice notes, given you credit, or offered a compliment that you can put in an Encourage-ment File, I have a solution. Write yourself some nice letters. Write down what you like about yourself. List your strengths. List your accomplishments. List some of the good things you've done for others.

It's okay to encourage yourself because that's what God did. He praised Himself. We're told in the book of Genesis that God created the waters and He said, "That was good." He created the sky and He said, "That was good." He created the fish and the animals and He stepped back and said, "That was good." He created you and me and said, "That was really good."

I love the fact that God praised Himself. Most of the time we are so critical of ourselves, and so focused on what we've done wrong, we never even think about complimenting ourselves.

*I've got these faults. I'm struggling with this addiction.* Or, *I'm not nearly as talented as my co-workers.*

That's not the way to think. Find something that you're doing right so you can say, "You know what? That was good."

Even when you walk out of church, you can pat yourself on the back and say, "I did something right today. I took time to honor God by coming to church. I must say, 'I did good.'"

When I walk off the platform at Lakewood Church each week I

look at myself in the mirror and say, "You did good today." I may not have done as well as somebody else, but I did the best that I could do, and that's all that really matters.

Here's my point: If you don't compliment yourself, you will never become everything God created you to be, and you will never find joy in each day. To do that, you must feel good about who you are. I'm not talking about being arrogant and going around thinking you are better than everybody else. I'm talking about learning to accept and approve of yourself.

Happiness is an inside-out proposition. If you aren't happy with yourself, you will never be able to find joy in each and every day. Instead of always catching yourself doing something wrong, I want you to get in the habit of catching yourself doing things right.

## Consider This

Many times, after just five minutes of being reminded how much people love you and of remembering some of the good things you've done, your attitude will totally change.

---

---

---

---

---

---

---

All men dream: but not equally. Those who dream by night in the dusty recesses of their minds wake in the day to find that it was vanity: but the dreamers of the day are dangerous men, for they may act their dream with open eyes, to make it possible.

—T. E. Lawrence

_____

_____

_____

_____

_____

_____

_____

## What the Scriptures Say

The name of the LORD is a strong fortress; the godly run to him and are safe.

—Proverbs 18:10 (NLT)

They that wait upon the LORD shall renew their strength; they shall mount up with wings as eagles; they shall run, and not be weary; and they shall walk, and not faint.

—Isaiah 40:31 (KJV)

## A Prayer for Today

Father, thank You for loving me. Thank You for believing in me and always building me up. I ask that You show me creative ways to encourage myself and to build up the people around me. Help me to be an example of Your love today and always.

_____

_____

_____

_____

_____

_____

_____

_____

_____

To help yourself, you must be yourself. When you make a mistake, learn from it, pick yourself up and move on.

—Dave Pelzer

_____

_____

_____

_____

_____

_____

_____

_____

### Takeaway Truth

When nobody else celebrates you, learn
to celebrate yourself. When nobody else
compliments you, then compliment yourself.
It's not up to other people to keep you
encouraged. It's up to you. Encouragement
should come from the inside.

# DAY 3

## Listen to the Voice of Victory

. . . . . . . . . . . . . . . . . . . . . . . . . . . . . . . . . . . . . . . . . . . .

*Key Truth*
There are all kinds of thoughts and all
kinds of voices we can tune in to,
so choose the voice of victory.

. . . . . . . . . . . . . . . . . . . . . . . . . . . . . . . . . . . . . . . . . . . .

There are hundreds of different frequencies in the air right now all around you. If you had a receiver, you could tune in to station after station. In the same way, you can tune out a station. You've been in your car when a song or a talk show that you don't like comes on the radio. It's no big deal. You don't make yourself listen to it. You don't sit there and endure it. You just push a button and switch over to a different station. The same principle works with your thinking.

All through the day there are thoughts coming into your mind. Many of these are negative and discouraging thoughts, like *You'll never be healthy. You'll never accomplish your dreams. You'll never be married. You'll never overcome your problems.*

Many people are unaware that you don't have to stay on that station. Just because a thought comes doesn't mean you have to dwell on it. If that thought is negative, discouraging, or depressing, you simply need to tune out that frequency and find a different station or channel.

There's a channel I recommend called the "Voice of Victory." It originates from God's Word. It says, "You have a bright future." It says,

"You are blessed. You are healthy. You are forgiven. You have favor. You can overcome any obstacle. You can accomplish your dreams."

If you want to live in victory, in happiness and joy, stay tuned to the right channel. You can't go around all day thinking things like *I can't stand my job and I'm so overweight and I'm never going to get out of debt.*

Thinking those thoughts is draining your energy, your joy, your happiness, and your zeal. You are losing all the good things God has put in. You would be amazed at how much better you would feel if you got up each day and went on the offensive instead of being passive and entertaining every negative thought that comes to your mind.

Think positive thoughts on purpose. Get up in the morning and make a declaration of faith. Say out loud to yourself, "This is going to be a great day. God is directing my steps. His favor is surrounding me like a shield. I'm excited about this day."

When you do that, you will be stronger and happier, and you will see God's favor in a greater way. Pay attention to what you're thinking. Some people have been tuned in to the Worry Channel so long they could be lifetime members. They could own stock in that channel, they are so full of worries.

## Consider This

There is a better way to live. When those negative thoughts come, you have to make a choice to not dwell on them. Instead, use the arrival of negative thoughts as a reminder to thank God that He's at work. Just switch the channel and thank Him for changing things in your favor.

_____

_____

_____

_____

_____

_____

_____

_____

He who has learned to pray has learned the greatest secret of a holy and happy life.

—William Law

_____

_____

_____

_____

_____

_____

_____

## What the Scriptures Say

Since we are surrounded by such a great cloud of witnesses, let us throw off everything that hinders and the sin that so easily entangles. And let us run with perseverance the race marked out for us.

—Hebrews 12:1 (NIV)

The LORD your God is going with you! He will fight for you against your enemies, and he will give you victory!

—Deuteronomy 20:4 (NLT)

## A Prayer for Today

Father, open the eyes of my heart. Help me to see the grandstands of heaven cheering me on. Thank You for instilling confidence, power, and grace in me so that I can run my race and finish strong!

_____

_____

_____

_____

_____

_____

I count him braver who overcomes his desires than him who conquers his enemies; for the hardest victory is over self.

—Aristotle

_____

_____

_____

_____

_____

_____

### Takeaway Truth

When somebody does you wrong, there's a voice inside that says, *Get even. Hold a grudge. Never speak to them again.* If you dwell on those thoughts, they will poison your life. But there's another mind frequency you can tune in to. It says, *God is my vindicator. He'll make my wrongs right. What was meant for my harm, He'll use to my advantage.*

# Focus on the Good

*Key Truth*
You can select what you focus on, so focus on
the good and tune out the bad in your life.

I watched a television documentary about a jungle bat that eats certain small frogs, but not all small frogs. Some of the jungle frogs are poisonous. They look just like the nonpoisonous frogs. But this bat can tell the difference by the sounds made by the frogs. The bat tunes in to only the sound made by the nontoxic frog.

At night all the frogs make this high-pitched chirping sound, but the poisonous frogs chirp in a slightly higher pitch than the nontoxic frogs. These bats have hearing so keen, they just listen intently for five or ten minutes, and then they tune in.

The documentary showed twenty jungle frogs packed into a little bitty area. Then the jungle bat tuned in and swooped down. For its dinner, the bat picked out the one nonpoisonous frog in the midst of all its poisonous cousins. How could the bat do that? He had trained his ear to tune in to the right frog frequency.

That's the way to be when selecting which thoughts to tune in. Be so trained in your thought life that you don't take the enemy's bait. You tune in to only hopeful, positive, faith-filled thoughts.

When a jealous thought comes saying, *Why do they get everything?*

*They're so smart? That's not fair*, recognize that thought is making the wrong sound. It may look good, and you may be tempted to dwell on it, but your instincts should tell you that's a toxic thought.

If a thought comes telling you, *You're so sloppy. You're undisciplined. You can't do anything right*, it may be tempting to get down on yourself, but don't take that bait. Recognize those are poisonous thoughts. They will keep you from your destiny.

I'm asking you to be extremely aware of what you're dwelling on. What thoughts are you allowing to take root? Poisonous or nonpoisonous? Helpful or hurtful? Have you trained your ears to have selective hearing? Are you being perceptive like those bats to leave the poisonous thoughts alone?

You have to program your mind with the right software. If you'll keep your mind filled with the right thoughts, there won't be any room for the wrong ones. Purposefully think good things about yourself and your future. It's not enough to just avoid negative thoughts. If you don't fill your mind with these faith-filled thoughts, the negative ones will try to take over. It's much better to stay on the offensive.

The Bible says, "You will keep him in perfect peace, whose mind is stayed on You" (Isaiah 26:3 NKJV). Meditate all through the day on what God says about you: *I'm strong. I'm talented. I'm forgiven. Good things are in store for me. My best days are in front of me.* When your mind is full of positive thoughts, negative thoughts will find a NO VACANCY sign when they try to enter. They won't be able to get in. That is a powerful way to live.

## Consider This

When you keep your mind filled with positive thoughts, you choose blessings; you are choosing to live with happiness each day. You choose joy and victory. But when you are passive and accept whatever negative thoughts come to mind, that's when you miss out on God's best.

A pessimist is one who makes difficulties of his opportunities and an optimist is one who makes opportunities of his difficulties.

—Harry Truman

## What the Scriptures Say

Dear brothers and sisters, one final thing. Fix your thoughts on what is true, and honorable, and right, and pure, and lovely, and admirable. Think about things that are excellent and worthy of praise.

—Philippians 4:8 (NLT)

You will keep in perfect peace those whose minds are steadfast, because they trust in you.

—Isaiah 26:3 (NIV)

## A Prayer for Today

Father, today I choose to focus on You. I open my heart and mind to receive Your daily benefits. Show me ways to be a blessing to others and a good example of Your love.

_____

_____

_____

_____

_____

_____

_____

_____

_____

Become a possibilitarian. No matter how dark things seem to be or actually are, raise your sights and see possibilities— always see them, for they're always there.

—Norman Vincent Peale

_____

_____

_____

_____

_____

_____

_____

_____

_____

_____

_____

### Takeaway Truth

The key to accessing God's best each and every
day is to set your focus in the right direction.
You can't wait to see how you feel, what kind of
mood your spouse is in, what the traffic is like, or
what the stock market is doing. No, you have to
choose to set your focus by saying, "This is going
to be a great day. I am blessed and cannot be
cursed! I know God is directing my steps;
something good is going to happen to me today!"

# DAY 5

## *Detox Your Mind*

*Key Truth*

If you don't have joy, happiness, or victory in
your life, maybe it's because of an unhealthy
diet. Not physically but mentally. There is too
much mental junk food polluting your mind.

I have a friend who is trying to be healthier and he won't eat any kind of meat. He's not drinking anything but water. He won't eat after a certain time at night. I saw him the other day and offered him a soft drink, and he didn't think twice before declining.

"No, that's not a part of my eating program," he said.

He was on a strict diet. That's the way to be when toxic thoughts come to mind, those thoughts of worry, low self esteem, and *not able to* thoughts. When they arise just say, "Thanks, but no thanks. That's not a part of my plan. I don't dwell on thoughts of fear. I don't dwell on thoughts of defeat. I don't dwell on thoughts of inferiority."

I'm asking you today to go on a fast. Not a fast from food, but a fast from negative thinking, a fast from condemnation, a fast from resentment, a fast from *can't do it* thoughts, a fast from undernourished dreams. Starve those toxins. Do not give them any power over you. Every morning when you wake up, go through a mental cleansing. Release any bitterness, forgive the people who hurt you, and let go of every disappointment. Start the day in faith. Start the day believing. Don't let those toxins build up.

When you're lying in bed in the morning, just say to yourself, "This is going to be a great day. I'm expecting God's favor. I know I'm well able to fulfill my destiny. I've been empowered to overcome every obstacle. I have the strength to overlook every offense. I have the grace to rise above every disappointment. Even if things don't go my way today, I know God's in control, and I'm making up my mind right now to be happy and enjoy this day."

You are cleansing your mind. You are cleaning out all the toxins, all the negativity, and all the condemnation. During the day when opportunities arise to be offended, to be upset, or to be discouraged, don't accept those thoughts. Banish them from your daily mental diet.

If somebody is rude to you or offends you and negative thoughts arise, instead of dwelling on them, learn to say, "I'm not getting upset. I know this day is a gift from God, and I'm making a decision to stay in peace."

When you do that, you are staying with a healthy mental diet. That toxic thought can't poison you if you don't dwell on it.

A woman told me recently about the negative environment she grew up in. The people who raised her were constantly putting her down, and she didn't feel like she measured up to her sister. She couldn't seem to catch any good breaks and couldn't keep any good friends. She finally said, "It's like these people have cursed my future. It's been one disappointment after another."

I told her what I'm telling you: Before anyone could put a curse on you, God put a blessing on you. And no matter what they've said about you, no matter how they've tried to make you feel, the blessing always overrides the curse.

Get in agreement with God and start shaking it off. Just say, "Thanks, but no thanks. I'm a child of the Most High God. I am blessed and I cannot be cursed. I am surrounded with favor. I'm wearing my crown of honor. I'm equipped with everything I need to succeed."

I can see through my eyes of faith right now that your toxic thoughts are starting to dissipate. I can see strongholds that have held you back for years being broken. I can see you stepping into a new freedom, rising to a new level. I see you shaking off negativity and coming into faith. I see you breaking free from condemnation and stepping into confidence. I see a mind-set of poverty and defeat giving way to an abundant life mentality. As you get rid of those toxic thoughts, God will take you places you've never dreamed of.

## Consider This

Always remember that you are not who people say you are; you are who God says you are. People may say you'll never be successful, but God says whatever you touch will prosper.

_____

_____

_____

_____

_____

_____

_____

Change your thoughts and you change your world.
—Norman Vincent Peale

_____

_____

_____

_____

_____

_____

_____

## What the Scriptures Say

May all my thoughts be pleasing to him, for I rejoice in the LORD.

—Psalm 104:34 (NLT)

We demolish arguments and every pretension that sets itself up against the knowledge of God, and we take captive every thought to make it obedient to Christ.

—2 Corinthians 10:5 (NIV)

## A Prayer for Today

Father, today I choose to take captive every thought. I choose to renew my mind according to Your Word. Holy Spirit, thank You for being my teacher and helper. I invite You to direct me in the way that I should go. Help me fulfill my destiny.

_____

_____

_____

_____

_____

_____

_____

Everyone should keep a mental wastepaper basket and the older he grows the more things he will consign to it—torn up to irrecoverable tatters.

—Samuel Butler

_____

_____

_____

_____

_____

_____

_____

_____

_____

. . . . . . . . . . . . . . . . . . . . . . . . . . . . . . . . . . . . . . . . . . . .

### *Takeaway Truth*

Self-defeating thoughts can rob you of your joy
and happiness, but you can choose to eliminate
them from your daily mental diet. I want to
challenge you today to think about what
you're thinking about. Don't let those self-
defeating thoughts linger in your mind.
Instead, speak God's promises over your
life. Declare what He says about you.
Take captive every thought and renew
your mind daily. As you do, you'll be
empowered to move forward into the
abundant life He has for you!

. . . . . . . . . . . . . . . . . . . . . . . . . . . . . . . . . . . . . . . . . . . .

# *Don't Let Anyone Tell You Who You Are*

*Key Truth*

You have the power to define yourself according
to God's plan for you.

Henry's parents moved from Germany to the United States a
few years before he was born. The father was an international busi-
nessman and very successful. He wanted the boy to join him in
business one day. But Henry struggled terribly in school. He tried
and tried, but he had great difficulty in reading and writing and
arithmetic. His mother and father were hard on him. In German,
they called him a "*dumm hund*," which translates to "dumb dog."

Henry's severe dyslexia would not be diagnosed until he was in his
thirties, so he was devastated by their harsh words. He grew up insecure,
thinking he was stupid. The only thing that saved him in school was a
sense of humor. He was good at making the other kids laugh.

Henry became popular with the other kids. He really shone in his
speech and drama classes so he pursued those subjects, much to the
horror of his parents. They thought he'd never amount to anything.

Of course, they changed their minds after Henry rejected their
definition of him and defined himself instead. They couldn't believe
it when their insecure boy graduated from Yale Drama School and
became the star of a hit television show by playing a tough high
school dropout.

It was ironic that the name of his first big show was *Happy Days*, because Henry Winkler, now a famous actor, writer, director, and producer, really does remember those days on his first hit television show as some of the happiest of his life. Those were the days when he finally rejected the toxic thoughts of others and became the talented and creative man that his heavenly Father intended him to be. Henry focused on God's best within him, not on what others said about him.

Gideon had almost the opposite experience, according to the Bible. When God called Gideon a mighty man of (fearless) courage, Gideon looked around and said, "Who's He talking to? That's not me."

God had an assignment for Gideon, something great for him to accomplish, but Gideon had not renewed his mind. He had another image of himself. God saw him as strong, but Gideon saw himself as weak, defeated, and not able to.

God wanted him to lead the people of Israel and to defeat an opposing army, but Gideon said, "God, I can't do that. I'm the least one in my father's house. I come from the poorest family. I don't have the education, the skills, the courage."

Notice how Gideon perceived himself compared to how God saw him. God said he was a mighty man of fearless courage. If God were to call your name today, He wouldn't say, "Hello, you weak worm of the dust. Hello you failure. Hello, you ol' sinner. How's My loser doing today?"

God would say the same sort of thing to you that He said to Gideon: "Hello, Mary, you mighty woman of fearless courage." Or "Hello, Bob, you mighty man of fearless courage."

## Consider This

I believe in the coming days God will present you with new opportunities. New doors will open. New people will come across your path. Maybe there will even be a new career opportunity. If you are to reach a new level, you must be ready and able to define yourself as deserving of the best.

_____

_____

_____

_____

_____

_____

_____

_____

If you hear a voice within you say "you cannot paint," then by all means paint, and that voice will be silenced.

—Vincent Van Gogh

_____

_____

_____

_____

_____

_____

_____

_____

## What the Scriptures Say

The LORD will be your confidence, and will keep your foot from being caught.

—Proverbs 3:26 (NKJV)

The angel of the LORD appeared to him and said to him, "The LORD is with you, O mighty man of valor."

—Judges 6:12 (ESV)

## A Prayer for Today

Father, thank You for loving me and calling me Your own. I choose to receive Your Word, which is life, health, and strength to me. Fill me with Your peace and wisdom. I set my thoughts on You.

_____

_____

_____

_____

_____

_____

_____

_____

Nobody can make you feel inferior without your consent.
—Eleanor Roosevelt

_____

_____

_____

_____

_____

_____

_____

_____

_____

_____

_____

## *Takeaway Truth*

The question is, are we going to believe what God says about us, or are we going to believe what we feel, what we think, or what the circumstances look like? You may feel weak today, but God calls you strong. You may feel like a victim, but God calls you a victor. You may be afraid, but God calls you confident. Today, get into agreement with God. No matter what the circumstances look like, you've got to dig your heels in and say, "God, I agree with what You call me. I'm free, forgiven, and healed in Jesus' name!"

# Make No Apologies for Your Blessings

*Key Truth*

Your honor, joy, peace, victory, and happiness
have been earned at a price.

A gentleman stopped me awhile back and told me about bumping into my father on a street in downtown Houston back in the 1970s. My dad didn't know this young man, but he was at one of the lowest points in his life. He had just dropped out of school and didn't have any direction. My father came up to him and gave him one hundred dollars and said, "Young man, I don't know you, but God has got a great plan for your life. You keep moving forward."

That was a turning point in the young man's life. He went back to school and earned a degree. Today he is a medical doctor with a very successful practice.

When I wear my blessings, I'm not only honoring God, I'm also honoring my earthly father, who spent his life helping others. I'm honoring my mother, who has cared for so many. I'm honoring my grandmother, who worked tirelessly. I'm honoring my grandfather, who gave and served.

When you see me happy, healthy, blessed, and living well, I make no apologies. It's the goodness of God being passed from generation to generation. I won't downplay it. I won't make excuses. I know God takes pleasure in the prosperity of His children.

Our attitude should not be *Look at how great I am. Look at all I have.* No, turn it around: *Look at how great God is. Look at what the Lord has done in my life, in my family.*

## Consider This

All through the day we should be bragging on the goodness of God. We may not have deserved it. We didn't earn it. Many times it's just another handful of blessing on purpose. Now don't let some negative, judgmental, jealous person, or even your own thoughts, try to convince you to not wear the blessings God has given you.

If you will wear your blessings well, being quick to always give God the credit, there is no limit to where He will take you. God will make you an example of what it means to live a joyful, blessed, prosperous, and abundant life.

_____

_____

_____

_____

_____

_____

_____

God gave you a gift of 86,400 seconds today. Have you used one to say "thank you"?

—William A. Ward

_____

_____

_____

_____

_____

---

---

---

---

## What the Scriptures Say

The one who sows righteousness reaps a sure reward.
—Proverbs 11:18 (NIV)

There was not a needy person among them, for as many as were owners of lands or houses sold them and brought the proceeds of what was sold and laid it at the apostles' feet, and it was distributed to each as any had need. Thus Joseph, who was also called by the apostles Barnabas (which means son of encouragement), a Levite, a native of Cyprus, sold a field that belonged to him and brought the money and laid it at the apostles' feet.
—Acts 4:34–37 (ESV)

## A Prayer for Today

Father God, thank You for setting up a system that blesses me as I bless others. Show me how to sow righteousness today, and let me honor You in all I do.

---

---

---

---

---

---

You say grace before meals. All right. But I say grace before the concert and the opera, and grace before the play and pantomime, and grace before I open a book, and grace before sketching, painting, swimming, fencing, boxing, walking, playing, dancing and grace before I dip the pen in the ink.

—G. K. Chesterton

### Takeaway Truth

God's kingdom operates on a system of sowing and reaping. What you sow, you will reap. But when you sow righteousness by doing the right thing in the eyes of the Lord, you will reap a sure reward. That's because God Himself is going to pay you back. He is the One who will multiply you when you honor Him. Today, keep doing the right thing, even if the wrong thing is happening. Sow righteousness. Stay in faith; keep believing because He who promised is faithful. There's a sure reward in store for you!